WHAT™

B□X

Out-of-the-Box Thinking
for Career and Life

by Sean Griffin

First Edition

"The only boxes that exist are the ones you create yourself."

–Sean Griffin–

Table of Contents

The Courage To Be Creative

You Know More Than You Know You Know

If It Were Easy Everyone Would Do It

Living Your Mythical Journey

Never Give Up

Dedication

There are many times during life's journey when it can be very difficult to express full gratitude and appreciation to all of those people who have influenced the molding of one's ongoing life. During my life journey I have been blessed to have had many dynamic and profound interactions between some of the world's most brilliant and intelligent people. I am fortunate to live in a place where I continue to meet and interact with individuals from whom I am continually learning.

This book is dedicated to all of those people who have influenced my life positively, creatively, linearly, spiritually, wildly, whackally, negatively, historically or wonderfully. From these experiences *What Box?* thinking has emerged and I am forever grateful.

Writing a book is no small task, that is for sure. This book has been in production for over five years as of the writing of this dedication. It takes a team to make this kind of endeavor become a reality. *What Box?* would not have been possible without the hard work, inspiration, and dedication of Alice Fenton who, as a contributing writer, has edited and enhanced every page within this book. Thank you from the bottom of my heart for your continued partnership through the up and down times. Kristen Bergman, my amazing wife, who has been an energizing and balancing force in my life. Without your support this book would not have been possible. I love you for all time. Brad Vernon for providing his technological wizardry which enable the pages of this book to come alive. Rusty Fleming, for taking a risk and allowing me to write down my stories for people to read and reflect upon. Brian Ruth for never ceasing to encourage me and keeping the dream of writing *What Box?* alive. Sandy Boswell with her amazingly big heart and for being one of my biggest cheerleaders. The entire Chronicle of Grand Lake family for their grand visions. And last but certainly not least, my Mom and Dad for never ever giving up on this starfish.

This book is a testament to a universal truth that "anything is possible."

December 3, 2005
Zena, Oklahoma

Acknowledgements

A special thanks to all the people who have influenced my life and this work: Frank Interbitzen, Ted Cundiff, Gordon Rudow, Lissa Slean, Michael Munn, Stanley Krippner, Kell Kelly, Chuck Castellano, Jeffrey Kramer, Bob Fenton, Mark Yoslow, Paramahansa Yogananda, Benjamin Franklin, Tony Buzan, Ross Perot, Nolan Bushnell, Ita Golzman, Susie Chu, Harry Taxin, Jackie and Andy Miller, Joe Becker, Warren Hegg, Joe Lambert, David Sibbet, Jay Slean, Michiko Uramoto, Dr. Don Perrin, Marie Mackiever, Chris and Jeff Bui, Debra Burger, Kari Loomis, Mrs. Farmer, Heather Mackiever, Lisa Sobrato Sonsini, Ainslie Mayberry, Al Shugart, Fred Hoar, Michael McNeilly, Paula Wood, Willy Wonka, Tracy Dreger, Benny Hill, Gabrielle Rico, Anne Marie Harmony, John and Kort Van Bronkhorst, Susan Bernard, Joe Harris, Art Clokey, Joe Paul, Lisa and Kevin Toller, Gary and Marilyn Mann, Abraham Lincoln, The Beatles, Willis Harmon, Howard Hughes, Ted Turner, Arthur M. Young, Mike and Harriette Long, Lou Moskowitz, Leonardo DaVinci, Walt Disney, Bob Glass, Walter Calmette, The Ocean, Kathy Taylor, George Lucas, Susan Smith, Ben Henke, Sabine Watermann, Dali Lama, Michael and Anna Baines, Bob and Yana Livesay, Dave and Pat Jones, Davor Sorich, Abe Simmons, Chris Escobar, Craig Malina, Scott Poncetta, Lou Rodriguez, Rod Martin, Barney Davidge, my grandparents, and so, many more. I thank you from the bottom of my heart.

"People become quite remarkable when they start thinking that they can do things. When they believe in themselves, they have the first secret of success."

–Norman Vincent Peale–

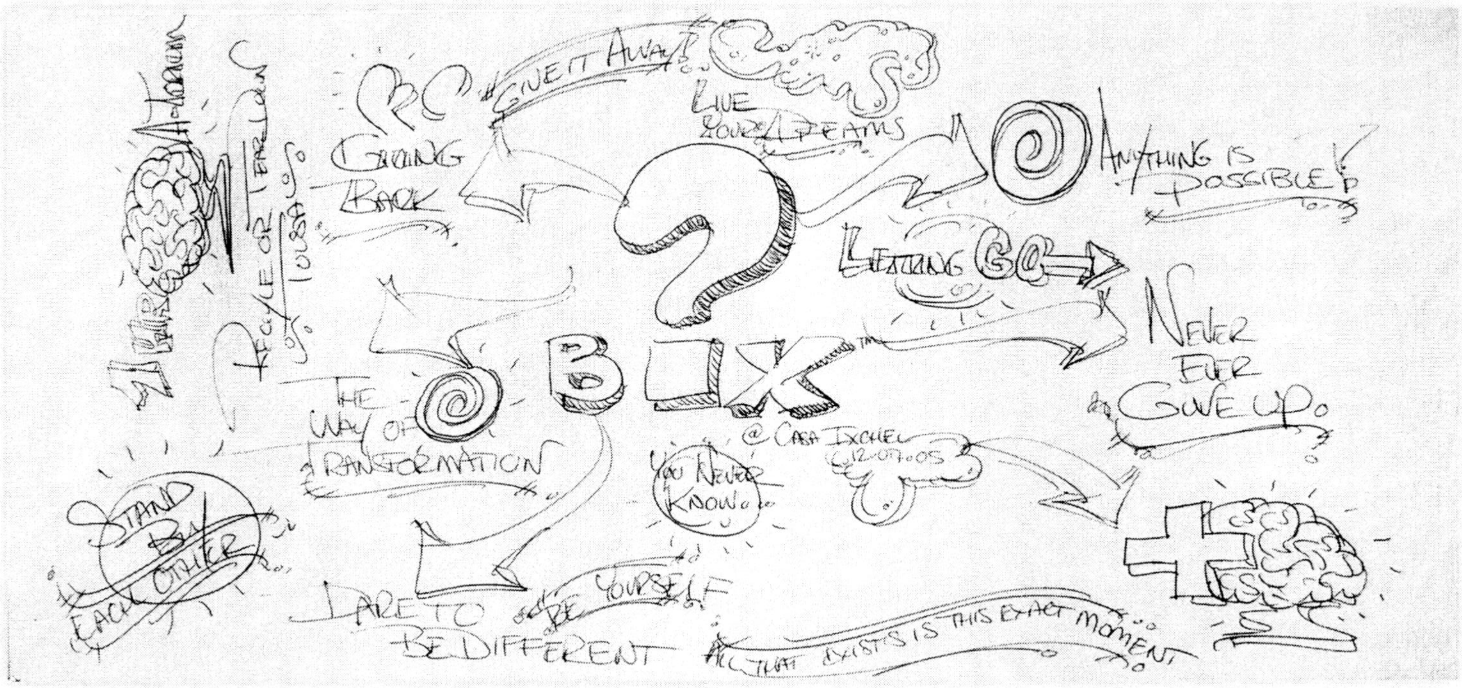
GIVE IT AWAY!
LIVE YOUR DREAMS
GIVING BACK
ANYTHING IS POSSIBLE!
LETTING GO
NEVER EVER GIVE UP
BIX
THE WAY OF TRANSFORMATION
@ CASA IXCHEL 12.07.05
YOU NEVER KNOW
STAND BY EACH OTHER
DARE TO BE DIFFERENT
BE YOURSELF
ALL THAT EXISTS IS THIS EXACT MOMENT

Welcome to What Box?

Even in the best and most supportive of circumstances the creative path is not an easy one. We can all recall times during our early years when our creative talents were shut down, leaving us thinking and feeling as if there was no possible way we could be creative or anywhere near as artistic as Picasso. Guess what? You are and you can.

The truth of the matter is that we are all made up of pure creative energy. Yet people have a tendency to dismiss, discount, and rob themselves of their most powerful essence, the characteristic which supports defining who they uniquely are as individuals, their creativity.

If you desire to increase your creative thinking and reach for your full potential then *What Box?* is for you. You may ask, "What is *What Box?*" More and more of us are being defined by the limiting parameters we set for ourselves, a box. People have them, communities have them, corporations have them, governments have them, and maybe even animals have them.

If we sit back for a few seconds and think about the idea of a box, we might see that some of the greatest discoveries in history have been uncovered by individuals willing to take a risk and think outside-the-box. Just by saying "I really need to think outside-the-box" we acknowledge that a box exists in the first place. What if there was a place you could turn and find creativity tools that would support your ability to be the best you can be, creativity tools that would support new and different thinking where there is no box? *What Box?* is the answer. This is a place where anything is possible, miracles happen, and where creativity reigns supreme.

Creativity comes when we view any given situation with a fresh and different perspective. One of our greatest keys to more fully accessing and utilizing our creative potential is a positive and open attitude. When we lock ourselves into old and non-productive paradigms we box ourselves in. My motivation and goal is to support you so that you can consciously exercise your creative muscles through with real-life stories of creativity and inspiration, along with creativity tools and exercises that I have researched, experimented with and created over the years.

Our dilemma is that we hate change and love it at the same time. What we really want is for things to stay the same and get better. *What Box?* can help to whack you out of your old and tired patterns with new and different thinking, allowing you to generate fresh new perspectives in all aspects of your life. As you explore *What Box?* your creative muscles will increase and you will start seeing the positive effects of a creativity as it emerges in your life. Together we will exercise the creative side of our brains and use more of our brain's potential. Some of the things we will explore include the art of visual thinking, how to embrace your creativity, keys to success, breaking out-of-the-box, the power of dreaming, creating the life you want, and how to unlock more of your full potential.

Your creativity is such a gift. When you begin to act on your creativity what you find inside of yourself may be more valuable than what you create in the external world. You have everything you need to be, all you can be right now.

Where do you want to go?

Is something holding you back from reaching for your creative potential?

What situation do you find yourself in that could use *What Box?* thinking?

Welcome to *What Box?* Let the adventure begin.

Breaking Out-of-The-Box

"Throw back the shoulders, let the heart sing, let the eyes flash, let the mind be lifted up, look upward and say to yourself, 'Nothing is impossible'."

–Norman Vincent Peale–

Breaking Out-of-the-Box

I can still remember my mother sitting me down one day and in a very serious moment saying, " Sean, how come it is every time I tell you not to do something you go and find a totally different way to do the same thing? What am I going to do with you?"

Now, I am not proposing that you go and change your middle name to "trouble." What I am proposing is that reclaiming your childhood vision is one of the best ways to start breaking out-of-the-box. In so many cases we have forgotten how to play, imagine, and, even worse we have forgotten how to be ourselves.

In 1968 a scientist named George Land gave 1,600 5-year-olds a creativity test used by NASA to select innovative engineers and scientists. Ninety-eight percent of the children scored "highly creative." Land retested the children five years later. Only 30% of the 10 year-olds scored in this category. By 15-years-old, just 12% of the adolescents tested "highly creative." And when Land gave the test over a period of years to 280,000 adults, he found that only 2% fell into the "highly creative" category. "What we have concluded," wrote Land, "is that noncreative behavior is learned." Wow!

> *"Every child is an artist. The problem is how to remain an artist once he grows up."*
>
> *–Pablo Picasso–*

Why is it that we tend to lock ourselves into paradigms, ways of thinking, that prevent us from thinking outside the box? Anyone who spends any quality time with children has at one time or another witnessed their natural ability to see the extraordinary in the ordinary. Their imagination is in all its glory, where anything is possible and play is their great passion. Children see the world differently because they have not been influenced by the outside constraints of our increasingly complex society. Daily routines, predictability, television, boredom, and mental plaque only support constricting our creative and innovative abilities.

As adults, thinking with childlike vision is hard work and takes courage. In many cases it means you may have to sacrifice long held beliefs, paradigms, to gain new perspective. If this is hard to believe, check out these classic examples from history. In 1899, the U.S. Patent Office Director announced that "Everything that can be invented has been invented." Then he requested that the patent office be shut down. Just twenty-eight years later, Harry Warner, president of Warner Brothers, asked, "Who wants to hear actors talk?"

Children are not afraid to try new things and fail because they believe anything is possible. They learn very quickly from their failures and apply those lessons to their next experiment. Failure can be one the most effective ways to break out-of-the-box. When we are not failing we are not stretching ourselves and only continue the patterns of doing the same drab thing we have been doing all along. When you fail and learn from those failures you grow and so do your creative abilities.

> *"Success and failure. We think of them as opposites, but they're really not. They're companions – the hero and the sidekick."*
>
> *–Laurence Shames–*

Like a wise sage that cannot be understood or whose lessons cannot be solved through traditional thinking, we have to ask ourselves puzzling questions to break out-of-the-box. How can I think more childlike once again? How can I add play to my life? How can I break free of the constraints of society? How can I learn to embrace failure and change?

Our children have the answers. When you get back in the sandbox you do too.

Tools for Breaking Out-of-the-Box

What Box? thinking has to be practiced all the time. Here are few ways to exercise your creativity muscles.

Transform Your Brain Into a Sponge

Think about this for a second. Like a computer humans only use 8-12% of their brain's potential. That leaves a lot of room for improvement. Next time you are in need of a creative solution, bombard your brain with relevant information. Speak to experts, read books, search the Internet, watch videos. Noodle it around and see how your conscious and unconscious work to support *What Box?* thinking.

Have Sheer Fun, Play

> *"Maturity means reacquiring the seriousness one had as a child at play."*
> *—Friedrich Nietzsche—*

Get yourself into some mischief because it stimulates creativity. One of my favorite places to play is a toy store. Have fun with the toys that make you laugh, think and in general have fun. Buy what makes you feel like a child again, Twister, bubble machines, maybe a water slide. If you were to visit my studio you would find toys all over my space. Keep toys and fun things in your workspace as a way to remind yourself not to take life to seriously.

Daydream The Day Away

> *"Everything starts as somebody's daydream."* *—Larry Niven—*

Have you ever been caught daydreaming and been told how unproductive it is to just sit and do nothing by daydreaming your day away? Turns out that daydreaming can be one of the more effective ways to solve problems or to invent things. Thomas Edison would actually make time each and every day just for daydreaming. Next time you need some creative ideas quickly, find a quite space, close the door to your room or office, get comfortable and let your mind wander. Who knows what great ideas you will come up?

Take Regular Breaks

> *"The time to relax is when you don't have time for it."*
>
> *–Sydney J. Harris–*

The ability to slow down and pause will allow you to see that which you might miss otherwise. Frustration, dullness and fatigue are some of creativity's greatest enemies. They are also giving you the clues to take a break. You can increase your creativity by taking a peaceful walk, focusing on your breathing patterns, or visiting an inspiring nature environment. Take a power nap. Thomas Edison would sit in an armchair his hands extended holding heavy objects in each. When the objects would fall and wake him, Edison would jot down the first thoughts that came to his mind. When you take breaks you allow your subconscious mind to do its creative work. Your subconscious is always working for your greater success. Trust it and take breaks regularly.

Ignore the Nay Sayers

> *"Excellence is attained when you care more than others think is wise; risk more than others think is safe; dream more than others think is practical; expect more than others think is possible."*
>
> *–Jim Gentil–*

Not much is more delicate and sensitive than a fresh idea. Nay Sayers are those people who discourage new ideas before they get the chance to be nurtured and developed. Protect your ideas from the Nay Sayers who tell you "It won't work" or "That's not in the budget." Take some time and share your creative concepts only after you have them more fully developed.

> *"Twenty years from now you will be more disappointed by the things you didn't do, than by the things you did do. So throw off the bowlines! Sail away from the safe harbor. Catch the trade winds in your sails. Explore, dream and discover."*
>
> *–Mark Twain–*

Letting Go of Fear

Fear is one of those things that we all have in common. At one point or another we have all been fearful of something: first days at school, starting a new job, change, walks in the woods at night, not being liked, big corporations, small towns, water, heights, change of any kind, and the list goes on and on. In all actuality fear is a very natural built-in instinct that served as a survival mechanism when we were hunter/gatherers, living from the earth having to fending off who knows what dangers that existed. The environment in which we live has changed a lot for us since those early days. Fear is one thing that has not changed.

Today our fears tend to prevent us from reaching our full potential by causing us to react in ways that, in most cases, do not serve us well. Fear suppresses our inner abilities leading us to continue to avoid taking risks in life. Let's face it. Living life is a risky business. If we spent half as much time learning how to take risks as we spent avoiding them, we would eliminate many of the fears that we have in our lives.

The things we fear most in life–change, fluctuations, disturbances, imbalances, and the unknown–are some of the primary sources for us to discover and unleash our creativity. The challenge is for us to acknowledge our fears and learn to use them to our advantage.

We see opportunities every day for people to step-up and take a risk and reach for something greater than what was only to be overcome by fear, and as a result sink back into their old patterns. The more you continue to repeat the same patterns the deeper those patterns become and the harder it is to change them. It's not easy that is for sure. Fear is a powerful force in our lives. Fear has the power to control you, if you let it.

There are ways to break out-of-the-box and to let go of fear. Instead of letting your fears control you, turn it around by embracing, learning and growing them. One of the first steps you can take in overcoming your fears is to face them head on. Over the years I have written many a page on my fears, and this is quite possibly the best first step you can take as well. Go ahead and think about what it is you fear and write it down. The pages are for you eyes only. If you are afraid to write down your fears don't worry. Remember, you are taking the first step in overcoming them.

"Let me assert my firm belief that the only thing we have to fear is fear itself."

– Franklin D. Roosevelt–

In all reality letting go of your fears is a lifetime project, a project that is a key for you to reach your full potential and to create what you want for your life. Being afraid to start something new is very natural and does not mean that you should feel as if there is something wrong with you.

When Kristen and I decided we wanted to move to Grand Lake in Oklahoma after spending only five days there on vacation we thought, "What are we doing?" We knew we would be selling everything back home in Silicon Valley in California, packing up our belongings and leaving behind the life we knew to take on a new one. Boy we were scared. What would we do? How would our lives change? How would we be received by the Grand Lake community? Would it be as wonderful living on Grand Lake as we remembered it when we were just visitors?

Our leap of faith has served to only strengthen our conviction that we have nothing to lose by stepping into the unknown and reaching for the stars. The decision to move to Grand Lake has proven to be the second best decision I have ever made, the first being to marry Kristen. It is hard to imagine, but what if I had let my fears of moving to a small town on Grand Lake in Oklahoma hold me back? Would I be writing **What Box ?** Would Kristen and I have been able to create the positive impact we have for the community? Would we have discovered that California is not the only happenin' place on the planet? I doubt it. Whenever I am fearful or scared of something, I just have to remember Grand Lake and then I know that it is all going to be just fine allowing me to unlock the courage to face my current fear.

Take a long hard look at the list of fears you have written down. Think about what it is that you need to understand about your fears that will support you to overcome them. Ask yourself questions such as, "Why is this a fear? How can I face this fear? What is the worst thing that can happen to me if I face this fear? Where does this fear come from? How do I change the way I think about my fears?" Trust your first instinct answers. You know the ones that come to you in the blink of an eye. Write them down as fast as they come to you or whenever they come to you. Noodle these thoughts around because they will help you to understand and overcome your fears.

In most cases we are fearful because we don't understand something, whatever it is. The more we understand our fears and the root of why we fear what we fear the more chance we have to overcome these fears.

You can do it! It is never too late to start letting go of your fears allowing the person you truly are to shine like the brightest star.

> *"Courage is not the absence of fear, but instead the mastery of it."*
>
> *– Mark Twain–*

Marching to the Beat of
Your Own Drummer

How much less would our experience of the world be if Thomas A. Edison had not worked day and night on over 10,000 inventions, believing in the impossible? What if Michelangelo had not challenged his creative potential while painting the Sistine Chapel to make the invisible visible? What would our world look like if Abraham Lincoln had not given so much of himself to transform our way of thinking about this great country? How much different would our lives be if a group of visionaries had not stood for liberty and behind the ideals represented in the Constitution of the United States of America?

These powerful representations are only scratching the surface of those who have made a positive difference in our lives. By marching to their own beat and believing in the possibility of the impossible, these people showcased for us the power of change we have hidden deep inside ourselves. They demonstrated what is possible.

Anything is possible if we strive to be more than we are today, to be ourselves, and dedicate our energy to working hard enough to make it so.

> *"The only way of discovering the limits of the possible is to venture a little past them into the impossible."*
>
> *– Arthur C. Clark –*

Yet, why is it that society tries to suppress those who march to the beat of their own drummer and even work to have them conform to the norms of society? If it is those people who march to their own beat, that in many cases act as the catalyst for the positive change we desire, showing us what is possible, and inspiring us to think differently, then why do we try to have these people become more like the majority of our society?

It is not just your God given right to march to the beat of your own drummer and become the best you can be. It is your responsibility. The world needs your unique talents and wisdom to show the rest of us what is possible. Only you can do it. Do it for yourself. Do it for the world.

In my life I have always marched to the beat of my own drummer, sometimes at great cost physically and emotionally. When someone does not easily fit into an identifiable societal box it is easy to discount or misunderstand them. Marching to your own beat is a lot of work and perhaps this is why most don't do it. You discover yourself in situations that force you to stretch and grow constantly. Continual improvement is a must to meet the ever changing array of challenges and fears that are uncovered along the journey. Every slip and every fall is a lesson learned, an experience gained, from which golden grains of wisdom are the reward.

Let's face it. You have to be pretty tough if you want to march to the beat of your own drummer. Most of the time it is just easier not to.

How many things that we think and believe to be impossible would be possible if we encouraged and supported everyone to march to the beat of their own drummer? Why do some of us want to be more like someone else other than ourselves?

Like Leonardo Da Vinci, we can all gain from believing in the power of marching to your own drummer, in miracles, and that anything is possible.

Life is amazing. How are you marching to the beat of your drummer?

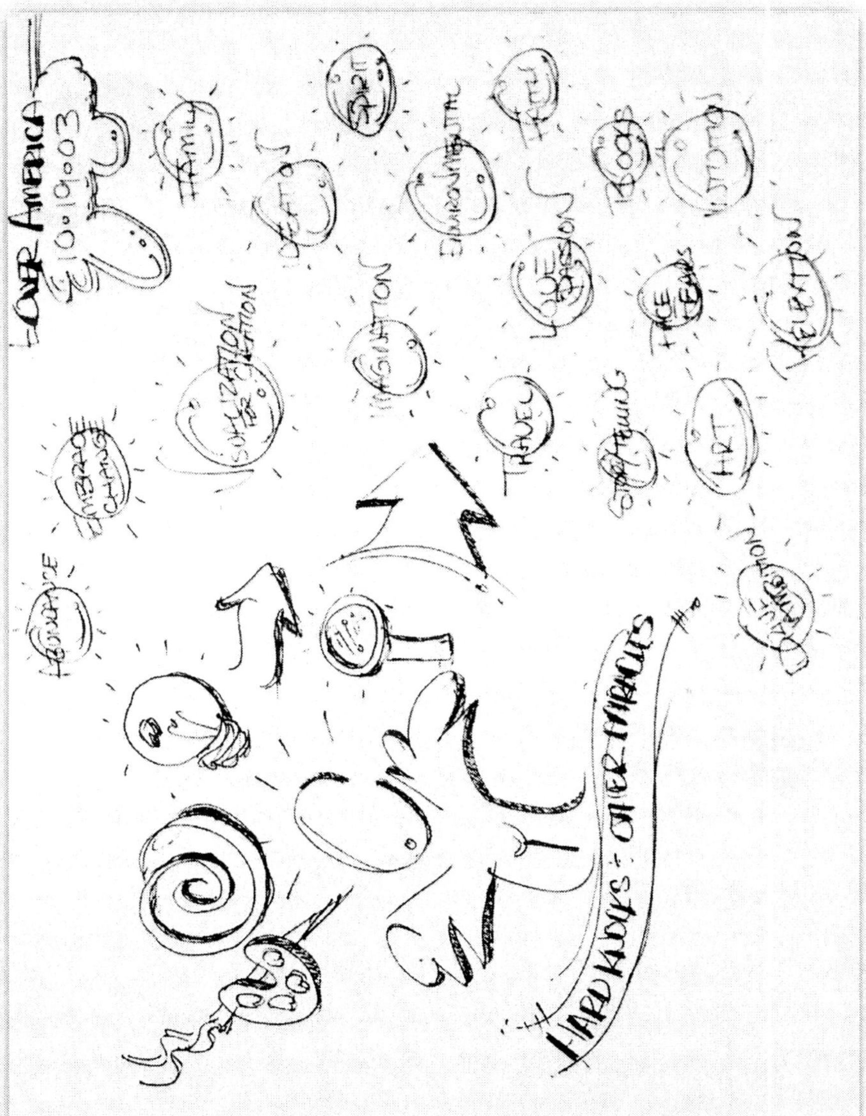
OVER AMERICA
10.19.03
FAMILY
BOOKS
TRAVEL
ART
HARDKNOCKS + OTHER MIRACLES

Discovering And Living Your Life's Purpose

"Life means to have something definite to do – a mission to fulfill – and in the measure in which we avoid setting our life to something, we make it empty. Human life, by its very nature, has to be dedicated to something."

– Jose Ortega Y Gasset–

Discovering and Living Your Life's Purpose

Discovering life's purpose is not a new concept. Since the beginning of time man has been searching for the meaning of life. Why am I here? What do I want? Who am I? Where do I want to go and how do I get there? Way down deep in our hearts we all want to find and fulfill our higher purpose.

Many of us have put our lives on autopilot. We eat, breathe, shop 'til we drop, work at jobs we hate and watch television. There has to be more to life than finding happiness and joy when the next American Idol airs or when buying the next trendy thing that only ends up in our closet collecting dust in a matter of weeks.

The whole idea of "I will be happy when. . ." is the way many of us live our lives. I will be happy when I make my first million. I will be happy when I own my house on the lake. I will be happy when I get that dream job. The reality is that happiness is not something that happens to you. Happiness is inside of you right now. Discovering and living your life's purpose will support you in living a much more fulfilling and happy life.

> *"Sow an act, and you reap a habit. Sow a habit, and you reap a character. Sow a character, and you reap a destiny."*
>
> *–Charles Reade–*

You are the architect of your own destiny; you are the master of your own fate; you are behind the steering wheel of your life. There are no limitations to what you can or can't do, have, or be.

So what does it mean to discover life's purpose? As one of my mentors, Mr. Rogers would say, "You are unique and special. There is no one else like you in the world." Because of this, each of us has a purpose and a reason for living that is uniquely personal. Living a life of purpose reflects who you are deep inside; your beliefs, your values and passion for living. It is all about following your heart and

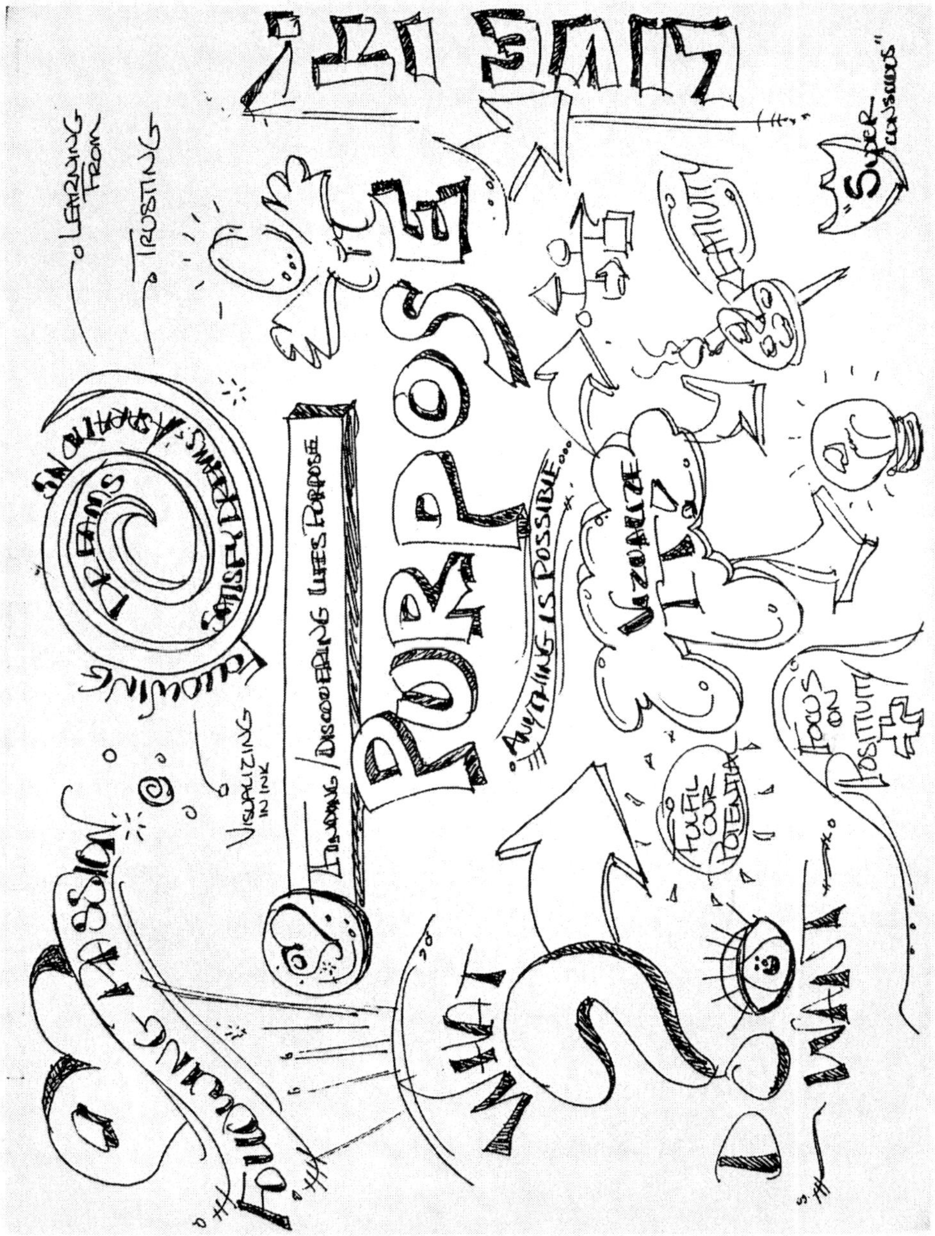
PURPOSE
FINDING / DISCOVERING LIFE'S PURPOSE
ANYTHING IS POSSIBLE...
VISUALIZE
LEARNING FROM
TRUSTING
VISUALIZING IN INK
DREAMS
FOCUS ON POSITIVITY
WHAT
WANT

doing what you love to do with passion and purpose. The Danish thinker Soren Kierkengaard wrote in his journal the following little gem. "The thing is to understand myself, to see what God really wants me to do; the thing is to find a truth which is true for me, to find the idea for which I can live or die."

Sometimes it takes a life altering experience to jolt us out of our superficial day-to-day lives and search for purpose. September 11, 2001 was just that life-altering day for many people around our great country and the world. Prior to that day many people were satisfied going through life doing the same old thing they had been doing for so many years before. The shock of the events that unfolded on September 11th caused many people to re-evaluate their lives and search for deeper meaning.

I happened to be in Manhattan on September 11th scheduled to facilitate a political town hall meeting at Windows on the World on the 109th floor of the World Trade Center at 8:30 am on September 12th. The town hall did not happen and I could not get back home to Grand Lake fast enough. As timing would have it, Kristen and I ended up rounding the corner at Kelly's Corner Store in Zena at the exact same time. As we almost hit the store running to hug each other, we cried and promised each other that from that day forward we would focus our lives on doing activities with meaning and purpose, activities that make a positive difference. We did and are doing just what we promised, but as that date slips into the cobwebs of history I find that I don't have that same passion in the belly as the first few months following September 11th.

Living a life with purpose takes constant practice, evaluation, and patience. Living a life with purpose does not mean that you have to be involved in some great discovery or tremendous idea. Instead, it often rises from a commitment to be faithful to even the most undervalued of tasks.

It is not all about going after the money. Instead, when we are doing work that adds value and improves the quality of life for others, we are doing life's work. Perhaps this is why people like to help each other. Subconsciously they know that through doing good for others they are coming closer to achieving their life's purpose.

> *"Leaders of the State of the World Forum determined that the most important jobs in the world are parenting, teaching, and healing. If you are parenting, teaching, or healing others, consider your mission among the most important in the world."*
>
> *–Laurie Beth Jones in The Path–*

How to Discover My Life's Purpose?

Life is about choices: good, bad, happy, purposeful or void. Living a life of purpose is a lifelong journey and there are many components that require considerable processing to live that life. Here are just a few creative exercises that will support you to start along your path to a life of purpose.

Follow Your Passions

Every one of us has in him a continent of undiscovered character. Blessed is he who acts the Columbus to his own soul! Get out a piece of paper and write down those things in your life that get your juices flowing and motivate you into action. Jot down all your passions no matter how out of this world they may seem. Now that you have your list, are you doing any of your passions or are they on the back burner? If you are already following through with some of your passions, how can you do more of what you love? If you aren't following through with your passion, how can you start changing your life and fulfill your inner most desires? When you follow your passions everything else in life will naturally flow to you and you will be that much closer to living a life of purpose.

Follow Your Intuition

> *"It is by logic that we prove, but by intuition that we discover."*
>
> *–Henri Poincaré –*

Whatever you call it, a hunch, a gut feeling, or luck, following your intuition will put the power of your subconscious mind and a lifetime of experiences to work for you. Just think of it as having your own personal advisor by your side at all times. And hey, it's you. When faced with a tough decision, take all the information you can find, no matter how large or small. Once you have sifted through the information, sit in a quiet relaxing space with this knowledge and see what pops up for you. What does your intuition share with you? What do you sense would be the best direction to go? Do any new and unexpected solutions come up for you? How will you use your intuition?

Remember, your intuition is always working towards your greater success and deepest desires.

Where Do You Want to Go?

> *"Vision is the art of seeing things that are not yet visible."*
>
> *– Jonathan Swift–*

Setting a vision for where you envision your life 20, 30, even 40 years from now is important in determining how it will turn out. Remember, every significant change or innovation began with a vision. So what is it that you want to accomplish in your life? Write it down and visualize it. It will give you a clearer picture of where your life is heading.

Focus On The Positive

"Nothing is possible if you think it is impossible. Nothing is impossible if you think it is possible. Think positive and work hard, and ANYTHING is possible."

–Thomas J. Vilord–

Keeping a positive attitude and approach to life may be one of the best methods for supporting you to live a life of purpose. Positivity is contagious. People want to be around people with a positive attitude. Positivity is like a magnet and attracts what it is you most desire in life and supports you to create joy in your life. What could be more rewarding?

The Art of Not Settling

I am constantly amazed at how many people continually settle for what is instead of what can be. It actually boggles my mind at times. One day at a meeting, when talking about a Civic Engagement endeavor, someone said, "Sean, what you are looking for is a Cadillac when a Chevy will do." No criticism to Chevy owners, I've got one. My response was, "A Cadillac would be nice, but what I am looking for is a Rolls Royce or Ferrari. And we can do it!"

Unfortunately, we see people settling more and more and it seems to be contagious, resulting in settling on top of settling. The time is now folks! Let's change the tide, turn the ship around, and carve a new path, a path where we are willing to compromise and at the same time unwilling to settle for anything less than the best that possibly can be. Our community, our state, our country and the world all depend on our ability to go for the best that can be and not to settle for anything less.

> *"Excellence can only be attained when you care more than others think is wise. When you are willing to risk more than others think is safe. When you dream more than others think is practical. And when you expect more than others think is possible."*
>
> *– Jim Gentil–*

Here is the challenge. When you settle for something less than what is possible the result is less than what you really desire. Settling can even have negative impacts that are totally unexpected. When you don't settle you come closer to setting yourself up for success instead of failure. If you do fail, and we all do, take notes, think about what you learned, stand back up, dust yourself off and get back on that horse.

When you think about it for just a minute, why would anyone be willing to settle for less than what can be? Is it because the goal is too much work? Is it because they really don't care? Is it because they would have to step up and put their ideals on the line? Is it because they might look bad in the public eye? Is it because they are empty inside? What is it?

Nothing of great historical importance has come from anyone who has settled. If ever there was a time in history not to settle for anything but the best for all people, it is now.

America would not be an example of what is possible if our founding fathers had settled for the status quo of English rule. NASA would not have gotten the space shuttle back to earth if they had settled and left the small pieces of mesh hanging from the under belly of the space ship. My mother would never have been able to have this non-traditional person educated if she had settled for me getting educated in the traditional school system. None of these people settled and it is my sincere hope that you won't either.

So what can you do to increase your ability not to settle in a time of so much settling? I have written and said it so many times before, "Anything is possible, and when we believe it and live it, this thinking will manifest itself in everything that we do." Ask questions like, "Why? How can we do better? Is there another way?" Keep asking questions until people begin to think differently. Offer up solutions, think-out-of-the-box. Never ever give up. Stay flexible and at the same time remain on task. Show what is possible by taking on the challenge. Take a risk. The biggest risk in accomplishing what you want in life is to not take a risk at all.

> *"Life is an adventure! Live it while you can. You can never have today again, tomorrow only comes once, and yesterday is gone forever. Make your choice wisely, then live the adventure you create."*
>
> *– Anonymous–*

What's Your Gift?

I have often found myself caught up in one of the outcomes of shopping leading up to the Christmas holiday known as "strip mall mania." This journey is not one for the faint of heart. The parking karma needed to secure a spot has reached new levels, and people can oftentimes be surly and rude. And the shear volume of advertising and media messages honing in like a magnet directed at our purses and wallets is enough to numb any mind.

It seems like we spend a lot of our time shopping for Christmas gifts and preparing them for presentation to that special someone. There is less time actually spent with the people we have bought gifts for, and even less when those gifts are sent to someone far away and unwrapped when you are not even present.

> *"The greatest gift you can give another is the purity of your attention."*
>
> *–Richard Moss, MD–*

What if there was a gift so special that you would not be able to find it in a mall, or in a boutique, and not even on the Internet? You would not have to shop away your hard earned money and time on things you or your gift recipients will not be using in six months anyway.

Inside of each one of us are tremendous gifts of talent and skill. The challenge is to consciously discover your special gifts and learn how to expand their capabilities and strength. I have found many of my gifts through interacting with people. When people continually and naturally act positively to the way I present, facilitate, or create, then I know that I am on the right track to more fully understanding my gifts.

I have also come to learn more about my gifts during down time. The time I take to visualize my ideas, rest on a couch, or walk in nature all give me time to see how to better grow and focus my energy on any particular gift I have. The challenge is that the more work I do the less time I have to go through these gift-building exercises. Even a few minutes here and there can make all the difference in the world.

When do people positively acknowledge you for your actions? What were you doing at the time? Could it be a gift waiting to be discovered?

As examples to think about here are some of the personal gifts I have given:

• One of my good friends in California was re-examining his career path. I shared the gift of life prioritization and future projections.

• As part of our family goal setting program, I shared the gift of facilitating, strategic planning and visual thinking.

• My father was working on a city council proposal to gain funding and approval to create a skateboard park in the city of Los Gatos, California. I gave my Dad the gift of group facilitation design and PowerPoint content development.

Giving the gift of yourself and your time is quite possibly the greatest gift one can ever give. The rewards on both sides are tremendous, going way beyond anything that could be bought. This does not mean that we don't have to go out and purchase gifts, because in some cases we do. It's all part of playing the game of life.

When it comes time for you to give someone a gift, think a little differently about the traditional gift giving you have done in the past. Instead, give the gift of yourself and your many talents to your family and friends. Just think of all the extra time you will have to spend with the ones you love and share your life with. Think of all the headaches and depression you will avoid. Think about all the money you will save, maybe for a rainy day. And while you're relaxing with friends, knowing you are giving the ultimate gift, you can only hope that, one day, the rest of the world shopping their time away will wake up and catch the "giving of your gifts wave."

Give it a try and see what happens for you and the person who receives your gift.

Good Still Happens

It is easy to get a little depressed with all the negative news being broadcast around the world today. Seems like every time I turn on the boob tube, which is not that often, news reporters focus on the negative and even appear to go out of their way to highlight the negative aspects of our society, e.g., another murder, child abuse, government corruption, the killing of seals, or a corporation manipulating the system by cooking the books. It is enough to make anyone lose a bit of hope.

This is why I am always on the lookout for the positive in life. You know, an example of what is possible when people focus on the good and work to make a positive difference in the world. While hanging out at McNellies, I met a person who is working to make a positive difference in the world. He has no expectation of receiving anything in return except to make a positive difference and, hopefully, inspire others to do the same. His name is Jeff Beasley and he has created a Web site called www.stillsomegood.com.

The inspiration for this Web site, and his desire to make a meaningful difference, came about because of what could be perceived as a negative event by anyone's standards. The house he and his wife were living in was flooded and as a result they had to move into a hotel for over a month with, get this, 2 children, 3 cats, 1 dog, and 1 lizard. Not an easy situation by any stretch of the imagination.

In addition to the frustrations of living out of a hotel for much longer than anyone would like, Thanksgiving was fast approaching. The whole ordeal had become overwhelming and I imagine things were getting close to the breaking point. One morning a total stranger walked up to Jeff's wife and handed her an envelope. Inside the envelope she found $60. Think about it. An anonymous gift of $60. How fantastic! It made her day. This simple act showed both Jeff and his wife the power that a random act of kindness can have on people, something we rarely see today. The family has never seen the individual again and has never had a chance to say thanks.

That random act, and Jeff's entrepreneurial spirit, was all it took to inspire him to figure out a way to inspire others to do the same and show that there is still a little good in the world. I just love it.

"Great opportunities to help others seldom come, but small ones surround us every day."

–Sally Koch–

Kristen and I have always been big believers in the power of random acts of kindness. We have bought dinners for people without them knowing it. We have paid bridge tolls for the next three cars behind us. We are big fans of the movie Pay it Forward, but we never thought of formalizing a process in which you can grow the possibility of others getting on the random acts of kindness band wagon.

I want to encourage all of you who read **What Box?** to visit www.stillsomegood. com and print up a few of the Still Some Good cards. They don't cost you anything and give so much back. Then go out and share the power of a random act of kindness. Buy someone a cup of coffee. Buy someone a lunch. Buy someone something that they really need. But here is the thing. Don't ever let them know you did it. Make sure to leave the card behind for the person who received the random act so that they can share their story with others on the site and motivate someone else to do the same. I can see the potential of this idea catching on in no time. Thanks Jeff. Keep up the great work.

"The everyday kindness of the back roads more than makes up for the acts of greed in the headlines."

–Charles Kuralt–

We can all make a positive difference. One star fish at a time.

Being Versus Doing

"Consciousness is not a state of doing but a state of being."

– Malcolm S. Forbes–

A Question of Balance

Just the other day, I was thinking, perhaps we might want to consider changing our name as a species from "Human Beings" to "Human Doings." Think about this for a minute. In Western society, we have become so active, that "doing" is the only way we seem to derive value from our lives. In fact, we are constantly developing new technologies and processes that enable us to do more things in less time so we can do more things. We are definitely in the "Human Doings" mode of operation.

And what are we "doing" all these things for? Will Rogers may have had a clue about why we are always in the "doing" mode. Will said, "Too many people spend money they haven't earned, to buy things they don't want, to impress people they don't know." And of course, spending more and more money means, "doing" more and more things.

As an artist portraying life issues, I believe that one of the main reasons we are always "doing," or in action, is because we have a deep desire to control things in our external world. We want to control our stature in life, the power we have, our leisure time, and security of our property, just to name a few. The reality is that control is merely an illusion and the more you attempt to control the more control you lose.

Technology, whether we realize it or not, permeates every fiber of our society and is probably the greatest single tool we have to enable us in achieving the control we so desperately desire. We put our faith, as a society, in the power of technology and the technical sciences to solve all of our problems. Having been deeply involved with the technology industry, I can see the potential danger with this kind of thinking. The danger is not with technology itself, but that it might become elevated to a religion or used exclusively as a tool to create profit. The inherent nature of a "Free Market" society is to develop competing technologies. The global arms race and terrorist threats that endanger all of us can be directly linked to this "Free Market" technologically-driven profit model.

Do you think that just because we have the power to do something we should do it?

Besides the noble art of getting things done, there is the noble art of leaving things undone. The wisdom of life consists in the elimination of non-essentials. Today, most people are so busy "doing" that they have lost touch with "being," and have become prisoners of time. As a result, our society has lost its sense of balance. This is where "being" comes in. "Being" implies being present in each and every moment and not preoccupied with what has happened in the past or what may or may not happen in the future. Taking the time to just "be" in nature, to focus on the clouds, to let the mind rest and to think of nothing opens up the possibility to create genuine wisdom. "Being" with your children, your family, and your friends without being preoccupied with what you could or should be doing will enable you to appreciate your life and your relationships with people in a meaningful and powerful way.

It is not easy to create a balanced life in today's world. As a society, we have collectively put so many expectations on ourselves that to come anywhere near achieving these expectations we have to keep on doing and doing and doing and doing some more.

Creating a balance in one's life takes tremendous effort. Life has its ebbs and flows and does not always follow the path we might want. You can take steps to create a more balanced life by setting aside time each and every day to do nothing and just "be." Take the time to appreciate your life and those of the people close to you. Take the time to rest your body and mind, creating a space to be in awakened rest and reflection. I have found that when I am able to incorporate "being" time into my day and life, I am better prepared to take on the challenges of life and feel more complete.

How often do you focus your energy on "being" rather than "doing?"

Living in the Moment

When it rains it pours and a few years ago it was pouring cats and dogs in my life. I had been sowing seeds on a number of exciting business, art, and community endeavors. And, as happens so many times, a bunch of these seeds of possibility had started to grow, all at the same time. These activities took quite a bit of energy to keep alive and I was starting to see myself running on the perpetual time-clock treadmill as my commitments continued to grow.

Just returning from San Francisco and a very hectic schedule, it was, indeed, good to be back home with my family, friends, and the sanctuary of nature. Taking a walk in the woods and along the lakeshore helped to relaxed me and slow down my thoughts. The urgency and stress of so much to do and not enough time to do it started to lift almost effortlessly.

> *"Presence is more than just being there."*
>
> *–M. S. Forbes–*

As I was wandering around my property I decided to sit on a bench surrounded by trees with a nice view of the lake. And while I was sitting there it happened. Out of the blue I became totally present in that exact moment. There was no past and no future in my thinking. I was totally absorbed by the leaves falling, spiders spinning their webs, squirrels busily stocking food away for the winter. The wind blowing through the trees created a beautiful song and I felt in tune with the rhythms of nature. I was living in the moment. I had no worries, no deadlines, and traditional time had lost it grip on my consciousness.

Then, just as suddenly, I was right back into thinking about the things that I needed to accomplish in the next few days. This line of thinking went on for a few minutes, then I consciously thought to myself, "Focus on the present, let go of the future." It took some effort and then all of the sudden I was back in tune with the rhythms of nature and totally present in the moment, no past, no future. This went back and forth for quite some time until I decided I needed a rest. I will probably be working on this one the rest of my life. Being present in the moment takes a lot of practice, because the present moment is very brief. It is instantly turning into the past.

This got me thinking about a workshop I have taught over the years which was designed to support the students to be more present in each moment of their lives. The idea is that for so many of us we tend to live our lives either thinking about the past, how we could have acted differently, reassessing past behaviors, wondering about "what ifs" or thinking about the future, where we ultimately want to live, the kind of job we desire, I would be happy if..., etc.

Here is the thing. All that exists is this moment, the right here and right now.

The Past is History

> *"I have learned that we cannot forget or throw away our past, but must not let our past control us either. We must learn and grow from our past failures, disappointments, and painful experiences, reset our goals and priorities and move forward. Start today by untying the knots that are limiting you."*
>
> *–Ty Howard–*

We can't change things and we can't go back in time, at least not that I know of currently. We can learn from the past but there is nothing we can do to change the past. It is in the past. Yet so many of us focus a lot of our mind space thinking about the past. If your past experiences and relationships have been positive, in all likelihood this is how you will project and think about future experiences and relationships. If you have negativity associated with the experiences and relationships in your past, this is how you are likely to think about your future.

When I think about the past I have a tendency to get stuck in, "I am not good enough. What will people think of my work? How could I have done it better? It will never work." When I think about the past in this way I am letting it take over and influence my behavior. When I relive the past in this way I am doomed to recreating the same thing over and over again. I have discovered through trial and error that consciousness of thought and presence in the moment support breaking these types of patterns.

When our minds are consumed by inner chatter we start acting like robots and continually repeat the same mistakes of our past without ever learning from them. The more you think about the same thing the deeper the groove in your brain and the more that pattern will continually repeat itself. Nothing new happens when we continually have the same thoughts and then we complain about what is happening in our lives. Your future will emerge as it always has been and the past will continue to repeat itself.

The Future is a Dream

"The best thing about the future is that it comes only one day at a time."

–Abraham Lincoln–

There is no way to predict what is going to happen to you today, in the next hour, or even the next minute. Anything can happen and we have no way of knowing what it might be. No matter how hard we think about the future it is a dream that we can't predict.

I know that I put a lot of my energy into the future: creating timelines for new business endeavors and projecting where they will be in six years; planning for what I will write for the next *What Box?* article; setting my schedule a year or more in advance. Because of these future projections I am setting expectations that certain things will happen and when they will happen. When they don't, I might get a little disgruntled and let the past creep in to support creating a future that has been repeated over and over.

"Whosoever doesn't know the past must have little understanding of the present and no vision of the future."
–Joseph S. Raymond–

Living in the present moment means being totally aware of what is happening around you, what you are doing, how you are feeling and what you are thinking. When we live present in each moment this does not mean that we give up learning from our past or stop developing plans for the future. Instead we are conscious, focused and present in the moment when we are making these plans and decisions. Living in this manner will support you to take on life's challenges with greater ease and deal better with whatever it is you are doing in your life.

By living more in the present you see things as they are, without the lens of your past or future. When you live in the present moment you start letting go of the influences of your expectations, agendas, fears, frustrations, desires, attachments, and history. You open up to new opportunities that might have been missed, because, maybe, you were dwelling to much on the past instead of being conscious of what was happening in the now.

You have the power to change by learning to live in the present moment. When you concentrate on what you are doing each and every moment, you gain the power of insight and the awareness of being alive. Through continual practice and experiential learning you start to realize the inner calmness, peace and release of thought that so many spiritual leaders have spoken about. You start to lift the veil of mystery and realize that presence in each moment is not out of our reach and, instead, is more like coming home.

Live As If . . .

What would you do if you were given the unfortunate news that you only had one day to live? 24 short hours. 1,440 quick minutes. 86,400 fleeting seconds. Would you spend your last hours with your loved ones? Would you fulfill the dream that sits on the back burner while life passes you by? Would you get depressed and give up hope? Would you travel to the place you have always dreamed of going? What would you do?

Guess what? None of us know how long we will be alive or when our number will be called. Each day is a gift and so many of us let time pass by without ever really thinking about what it is we really want to be doing with our lives. Life is so short why not live as if it is your last day every day?

It seems that more and more of us are settling for what is instead of striving for what can be. What dreams do you have? Do you work towards your dreams or do you suppress them in the back of your imagination because they seem too difficult to achieve? Our dreams challenge us to reach for our greater potential, they stretch us, they increase our creativity, they make us unique and they have the potential to become real.

180 seconds have passed since you started reading this *What Box?* piece. Time is ticking away. What are you waiting for?

Remember that dream you had as a child? You know, the one that is way back there in the cobwebs of your brain, the one that has been filed away under "never going to happen." It's time to pull it out and start working on it.

Dreams only happen when you work to keep them alive. No one said it would be easy.

In my life I work hard to keep my dreams alive and track those dreams that have come true. I have been blessed to have many of my dreams fulfilled: marrying Kristen, a remarkable woman with whom I have the privilege of sharing my life, visiting Machu Pichu, being CEO of a company, working in Hollywood, writing a creativity column, consulting with world leaders, creating my own schedule, and owning a slice of heaven on earth right here on Grand Lake.

"A dream is in the mind of the believer, and in the hands of the doer. You are not given a dream, without being given the power to make it come true."

–Anonymous–

What dreams have come true in your life? Write them down and appreciate what you have achieved. Now write down the dreams that have not yet been fulfilled. Write down your dreams, no matter how out of this world they may seem. You can make any dream come true once you set your mind to it. What is holding you back from achieving your dreams?

Another 360 seconds has just passed you by. Better get on it!

When you live a life that takes in each and every moment appreciating the positives and working towards fulfilling the dreams you have, then you are truly living. And what could be better than living life to its fullest?

There is no time like the present to "live life as if."

Wonder

When you think of wonder what do you think of? Something mysterious? Amazing? Awe inspiring? Overwheleming? Surprising? Or maybe emotionally charged?

Wonder is such an incredible part of being a human. Wonder allows us to understand that there is something out there way beyond and bigger than ourselves. Wonder has the ability to connect us to the source of all life, opening our hearts and souls to become more aware of our purpose in life, if only for a fleeting moment.

When was the last time you had a wonderous experience?

While sitting on the boat dock at our house in Zena, Oklahoma I have experienced wonder as the sunset fell over the trees. Whenever the vultures come to roost around our property I am in wonder with their beauty and graceful form. Driving the boat at night across Grand Lake almost always creates moments of wonder. While riding a boat from Cancun to Isla Mujeres I was in wonder as I viewed the detail of the ocean floor through the clear water.

Wonderous experiences have the ability to support the awakening of what it means to be totally present in the moment. A wonderous experience runs through every fiber of our being. It takes over all the stuff in our lives and only allows us to focus on that exact wonderous moment. It is a rare moment in life where there is no past or future, only the now. This is absolutely fantastic. I only wish I could sustain the wonder for longer periods of time.

How did your last wonderous experience make you feel? Grateful? Surprised? Like everything else just faded away? More connected to something unknown?

> **"By wonder we are saved."** *–Plato–*

When you are in wonder you are more open and as a result can experience more. During these wonderous times many people have new inspirations and awakenings. Life is all about wonder, enabling us to see ourselves as a part of rather than the center of the whole system in which we are an integral part.

Do you wonder?

Embracing Change
And
The Unknown

"One must never lose time in vainly regretting the past or in complaining against the changes which cause us discomfort, for change is the essence of life."

–Anatole France–

What's Your Groove?

Just like the vinyl LP's of yesterday the more you repeat the same patterns in life, the deeper the grooves of repetition become. We all fall prey to our daily routines and patterns. Some of them are beneficial and support our greater success and others only work to prevent us from reaching our goals and objectives. What grooves in your life would you like to keep and which do you want to change?

> *"Change is a challenge and an opportunity, not a threat."*
>
> *–Prince Charles of England–*

Like river water running over and smoothing the cracks in rocks and boulders it takes a lot of time and patience to smooth out our grooves. The longer the patterns have been played out the deeper the grooves, and the longer it takes to smooth them out so you don't play those grooves anymore.

It takes an awareness of our patterns to understand which grooves are good for us and which ones are not. Wearing down your undesirable grooves is not an easy task. In the end, the time and energy it takes to change and smooth the grooves is well worth the effort.

One of my deepest grooves in life has been my inability to face people and situations that have the potential to create confrontation. Throughout my life, the groove of avoiding confrontation had grown deep. Very deep. I had become so good at avoiding confrontation that I rarely had a problem with people or situations, at least on the outside. My insides were turning and churning and only those very close to me knew the pain and frustration I was enduring.

It was during my days as CEO of StudioFX that I was forced to face the fact that avoiding these potential confrontations, imagined or real, were not serving my company or me well. I had to do something to start smoothing out my groove of avoidance.

The question was, "How could I smooth out my groove of avoiding confrontation?"

"Without continual growth and progress, such words as improvement, achievement, and success have no meaning."

                                                                    –Ben Franklin–

I had a take a risk and confront the fears that were holding me back. I was scared. What would Golden Books Entertainment do when I let them know I would not be able to pay them any more money for the rights to the Underdog Show? How would CBS react when I let them know we had to have exclusive rights to the I Love Lucy Show or else we had no deal? I got way too tied up in what would happen rather than of focusing on what was happening.

The end result was that my insides stopped churning and burning. I found that the people I had been afraid to confront were much more receptive to my up front nature. It became easier and easier to face my issue of avoidance and smooth the groove so that it played less and less frequently. I continue to fall into my confrontation groove at times, only now the groove is so smooth that I am able to catch myself before I "skip" back into the groove.

We all have to pick and choose the grooves we want to change, the grooves that keep us from reaching our goals and objectives. What grooves do you have in your life that are holding you back?

Elemental P

This is one of those stories you just don't seem to forget. When Kristen, my wife, was a little kid, she, like many of us, learned the "ABC Song," in her case, while taking swimming lessons at the local YMCA. We all know this song–we sing along with any child who starts belting out the alphabet. However, there's one difference with Kristen's version. When she was stretched out on her back learning to float on the shoulder of her swim instructor and her ears were under the water the alphabet that she learned was a bit different. Instead of L, M, N, O, P, she learned it as a word instead of letters, "Elemental P." Imagine a small child singing the alphabet for years in school with all her enthusiasm and excitement, saying "Elemental P" Q.R.S.T.U.V. . . the incorrect letters and words as sung in the "ABC Song."

At the time, Kristen couldn't believe that she had gotten part of the "ABC Song" wrong. She became distressed and wanted to continue singing the song the way she had been prior to being discovered by a teacher's overly keen ear. After a while Kristen was finally able to accept the fact that she needed to relearn the "ABC Song" and say the letters L.M.N.O.P instead of her beloved "Elemental P." Sometimes mistakes such as the one Kristen experienced can leave lasting marks and effect how we act in our lives today. I think it's great that Kristen can laugh at herself and not take this kind of situation too seriously.

I would think that all of us have had more than our share of "Elemental P" experiences pop-up from time to time. Currently I am having my own "Elemental P" situation. My Macintosh PowerBook laptop computer recently lost the use of its "P". It's one of those letters you just don't think about a whole lot until you lose it. Words like "inspire" and "passion" have to be replaced with less impactful words such as "motivate" and "energetic." As a writer, the loss of "P" can be very frustrating, but also enlightening. I've learned to keep my Thesaurus at hand to replace words, I've created an entire Word document with "P's" written so I can cut and paste when I need one, and I've resorted to snagging my wife's portable keyboard for emergency use.

There are a number of steps I needed to take so I could discover the creative options that would solve my problem, if only temporarily. The steps that I took to arrive at alternative solutions went something like this. My initial response was denial, and we are not talking about the river here. "This just can't be happening to me. Not having a "P" available at my finger tips is holding me back from doing what I am trying to do." Then I started getting angry. "I just don't have time for this, damn it all." Then I thought, hey, I can bargain my way out this situation, "If I can just get this "P" to work, I will make this the best darn article I've ever written." As I sat there stumped by the whole thing I started getting a little depressed, "I really can't handle anymore obstacles right now and have too much to do." No matter how hard I tried to fix the problem, using the same tried and true methods, it just didn't work. Finally, after much time and mental effort, I was able to let go and acknowledge that what had been working wasn't working anymore. It is at this point that I started seeing new options and let loose my solution-based creative thinking, supporting me to identify new options. Once I arrived at this point, I was able to move past my anger and frustration to a place where I could be more open and see the creative options that would solve my problem.

> *"The difficulties, hardships and trials of life, the obstacles. . . are positive blessings. They knit the muscles more firmly, and teach self-reliance."*
>
> *–William Matthew–*

Do you have an "Elemental P" situation you're dealing with? How can you accelerate your ability to gain the creative solution oriented thinking needed to solve your problem?

Checking Out

Let's face it. Everyone checks out from the stresses of life in one way or another.

How do you check out?

Some people check out by taking their boats out on the lake. Others check out by hitting the local bars and drinking away their stresses. A growing number check out by sitting in front of their television or playing video games for hours and hours. Everyone has his or her own unique way of avoiding reality.

So, why do we have such an urge to check out?

Perhaps it is because of our hectic 21st century lifestyle. We have become over-loaded by the challenges to keep up and stay competitive in the game. This can create frustration in our lives and affect every aspect of our daily activities. In some cases the challenge in our relationships can compound our desire to check out. When you add work environments that expect more accomplishments with less time and resources life can start getting even more insane.

When we check out are we attempting to avoid something? How can we take responsibility for our actions and frustrations? When we check out are we avoiding taking responsibility for a situation we find ourselves in? Whatever is happening in our lives is a direct result of our actions or inactions and only we are responsible for this.

Here is the thing. The more you check out, the more you check out. It is just easier to check out than it is to check in.

You know what? There are times that I don't really want to write *What Box?* stories. I would rather check out, not do it and have some ice-cold beer. To be quite frank with you, many times it is a pain in my behind to come up with this stuff and meet the deadlines and demands of the publisher.

The truth is that I really enjoy writing these stories because it stretches me and aligns with my vision, mission and goals. What I really need is to take some time for myself, reflect and let inspiration take hold. This process is quite different from checking out because checking out is resisting, where reflection is about embracing what is really needed and taking responsibility. I choose to check in.

In fact, the world would be a much better place if we all checked back in. When we check in we start to face the realities of our situations and identify solutions. We see with greater clarity and gain new insights. This process empowers us to over-come adversity and create greater possibilities in our lives. I am not saying this is easy. Remember it is easier to check out. When you face your fears and challenges head on by checking in, anything becomes possible.

> *"Consult not your fears, but you hopes and dreams. Think not about your frustrations, but about your un-filled potential. Concern yourself not with what you have tried and failed in, but for what is still possible for you to do."*
>
> *–Pope John XXIII–*

The time is now to check into the hotel of life. How long 'til you check back in?

I Don't Know What I Don't Know

"All I know is what I read in the papers." —Will Rogers–

Eighty years later it could be said, "All I know is what I read on the Internet." I start each day with a regular routine of reading the New York Times, Washington Post, Wall Street Journal, San Jose Mercury News, The London Times, select headlines in The Drudge Report and yes, even The Chronicle of Grand Lake. The great thing about this is that I am able to do my daily reading by simply jumping on the Internet, wherever I am in the world. I wonder what Will would have to say about our technological advances of today.

If it were not for the Internet, Kristen and I would have not been able to move to Oklahoma because our core business activities have been so dependent on the Internet for our livelihood. Moving to and living on Grand Lake is the single greatest move Kristen and I have made together. On our weekends at our home on Grand Lake, we still pinch ourselves when we take our morning walks down to our boat dock and enjoy a cup of coffee together watching the wildlife, breathing in the fresh air and realizing how blessed we are to be living in one of the most special spots on earth. But if you would have asked us just five years ago if we would ever consider visiting much less living in Oklahoma we would have, in all likelihood, laughed our you know what off.

> *"What I admire in Columbus is not his having discovered a world but his having gone to search for it on the faith of an opinion."*
>
> *–A. Robert Turgot–*

We were both guilty of not knowing what we didn't know. What I have learned from this life altering experience of visiting and living in Oklahoma is that many of my opinions and beliefs have been based upon a lack of information and knowledge. Yet I have had a tendency to hold tight to these beliefs even when I have been totally wrong. I still catch myself doing this and have to remind myself that I may not have all the information to be holding onto these beliefs. The Oklahoma experience helps to keep this reminder strong.

What beliefs and opinions are you holding onto that may not be true? How can you gain information and experience to acknowledge that things may different than you think they may be?

Prior to visiting and moving to Grand Lake all I really knew of Oklahoma was what my mother had told me about our Great Grannie Arant. She lived in No Man's Land when it really was just that–that is prior to Texas giving it up to Oklahoma. She showed me old torn pictures and would share stories of how hard life was and how Oklahoma is a place no one would want to live. Of course there was The Grapes of Wrath, which has done nothing to help our great state overcome its image as a dust bowl.

Since moving here Kristen and I have traveled all over Oklahoma including places like Guymon, Lawton, Woodward, Oklahoma City, Norman, Nowata, Guthrie, Claremore, Tulsa, Quartz Mountain Resort, and many places in between. What we have discovered is that Oklahoma has influenced more of the culture of our nation than is realized by most people. From Tulsa once being the oil capitol of the world, to becoming one of the country music capitals of the world. Oklahoma has contributed to the culture and prosperity of the United States. When my father was named after Will Rogers I bet he never thought that I would move so close to the place his namesake once called home.

There are many examples we can all come up with where we did not know what we did not know and yet we have held strong to those beliefs and ideas. We have the opportunity and the ability to challenge those beliefs and get to what is real. Sometimes it is just easier to hold onto our long-held beliefs instead of exploring deeper and gaining a new perspective. Our country was founded by people who were willing to look beyond what was in front of them and then take the risk to move into the new.

How can you look beyond what is and what was to create something new and to gain greater knowledge?

The Power
of
Visual Thinking

"Vision is the art of seeing things that are not yet visible."

–Jonathan Swift–

Your Amazing Imagination

How often do you fantasize about your future? Do you daydream about something you want to create in your life? What about creating movies in your mind?

When you are using your brain to think up any of these things you are using the power of your imagination. Your imagination may be one of the most potent creativity tools you have. Whenever you imagine something you want to create in your life you are actually taking the steps to make that imagined visualization a reality.

When you use your imagination you are creating a mental picture of something that is not perceived through the traditional senses. Your imagination is so powerful that you can create the experience of a whole new world inside of your mind. Think about this for minute. Your imagination has no limits, no barriers; anything you think up is possible.

Your imagination is not limited to only viewing mental images. You can actually sense and feel sounds, smells, tastes, a physical sensation or experience emotions. When you practice using your imagination you start to unlock one of the great doors to making your dreams a reality.

> *"Imagination is more important than knowledge."*
> *–Albert Einstein–*

My good friend and mentor Mike Munn, former head physicist for Lockheed, would go out into his car and sit imaging solutions to his challenges whenever he was stumped. By getting away to a quite place where he could let his amazing mind wander he would solve problems related to satellites and rockets. He would always tell me, "Use your imagination to create anything you want in your life or solve any problem." Good advice.

The real key to turning your imagination into reality is "acting as if" the imagined scene were real and already accomplished. Instead of pretending it is a scene of the future, imagine it as though you are truly experiencing it in the present. Think of it and believe that it is an event happening NOW. Over history many great minds have told us, "Whatever you believe you become." If you believe what you imagine with all your heart and soul, what you imagine has the potential to become reality.

Here is the challenge that many of us have. We tend to look at our lives through a scarcity mentality. That is we look through eyes that fail to see what we don't have and we attach our imaginations to what we don't have. Remember, what you imagine is what you create. If you imagine scarcity you create scarcity. Instead, open your eyes to abundance, that you have and attract everything you need and desire in your life. This simple shift in thinking and imagining can have a profound change on your life.

A developed and powerful imagination does not make you a lazy daydreamer or impractical. No way. Instead your imagination strengthens your creative abilities and supports you to achieve what you want to create in your life. How amazing and it does not cost you a single penny. You have it, everyone has it. How are you using it?

When you start to practice and experiment with your imagination focusing on what can be, the positive, and abundance you start to put the power of imagination to work for you and the benefit of others.

This powerful creativity tool cannot be underestimated. You can prove it to yourself by taking one thing that is very important to you and imagining it as real in your life. Keep with it, imagining whenever you have a quiet moment. You have nothing to lose and everything to gain by applying this underutilized gift. Your creative abilities will blossom and flourish the more you imagine and believe what you are imagining. Don't let anyone tell you it does not work. Experiment with it and never, ever give up. The world you imagine is waiting for you to create.

The Art of Shared Vision

Anyone reading **What Box?** has the vision to see the written words on these pages, the environment in which we live and the people around us. Some of us might even have 20/20 vision or better. Maybe we have Eagle Eyes. In most cases, people have the vision to see what is in front of them.

The challenge is for all of us to gain the courage to discover a "vision" for our lives and for that of our community, our state, our nation, and the world that is beyond what we can currently see, a vision that improves life for all of us, for the whole system. Although before I was born, the power of John F. Kennedy's vision to put a man on the moon still lingers as one of the greatest visions of all time. It was considered a crazy goal for many years and then people of the U.S. became enrolled in the vision and started believing it could happen. This resulted in one of the most memorable "shared visions" in modern times. The outcomes of this shared vision include tremendous technological advancements that have made our lives better and more productive. We continue to feel the ripples from the success this shared vision generated.

How long has it been since you have been inspired and motivated by a grand vision? A shared vision? Throw out the Rule Book. All it does is support keeping you in the same place you have been. Think up a vision no one has ever thought of, a vision that will positively affect the whole. Write it down. Post it. Get excited about it. Refine it. Share it with family and friends. Start living it. Go for the brass ring!

How do we learn to see beyond what is in front of us and create a vision for the future? You know, a "Great Big Outrageous Vision" that supports the "whole" not only the self. Only when we move away from a life of mere existence for only "me" can we start to harvest the wisdom to generate a "Great Big Outrageous Vision" that inspires and motivates a better life for all.

The Six Nation Iroquois Confederacy lives by this vision. "In every deliberation we must consider the impact of our decisions on the next seven generations." Wow! To really take on the intensity of Iroquois thinking, we need to be thinking over 150 years out into the future. In all actuality, given the accelerated pace of technological change, we really need to be thinking more like Leonardo Da Vinci. That is to be thinking an amazing 500 years out into the future.

Our world is getting smaller by the day. Any vision, be it for a city, state, or country requires us to think about the generations ahead and how to enroll the local and global world into our "Great Big Outrageous Vision." It is about creating a shared vision that people can get excited about, one that enrolls the collective whole of a community, city, state, nation and the world.

If any vision is going to take flight, it needs to become a "shared vision." Creating a shared vision today takes courage. It has to be a big vision, one that is capable of being achieved in a tangible and meaningful way. It has to stretch the status quo with progress clearly communicated. Any vision needs strong leadership to keep the vision alive along the journey of ups and downs. People have to have trust in the leadership and their ability to generate the energy and talent to hold onto the vision and make it an integral part of their decisions.

More than ever communities, cities, states, nations and countries are in need of "Great Big Outrageous Visions" that support the whole and create a better life for all, not just a select few.

What "Great Big Outrageous Vision" is inside of you? It is time to set it free.

Create Your Life Your Way

How many of us are looking for more meaning and purpose in our lives?

How many of us are just going through the motions in our daily lives?

How many of us are willing to go through the journey to discover our greater purpose?

NOW is the perfect time to start the process of kicking butt with your life! You can begin by thinking about the kind of future you want to create for yourself. I truly believe you can create, in your life, whatever it is you desire the most. Thinking and visualizing positive thoughts about whatever it is you most desire will, in time, create that which you think about and focus energy on.

Ringing in the New Year is an extremely powerful time for people all over the world to set new visions and goals. In my life, it is the time of year when Kristen and I take the time to review our successes and failures, take in the lessons learned and then apply them to our updated life design.

> *"I know of no more encouraging fact than the unquestionable ability of man to elevate his life by conscious effort."*
>
> *–Henry David Thoreau–*

I started the process of brainstorming and visualizing personal goals and objectives on large pieces of paper sometime during my early childhood. Developing a collection of the visual history of my life has become an important tool to support a greater understanding of how my time and energy is focused. Focusing my time more effectively is one of my greatest challenges and one I am constantly working on. Envisioning the future and setting goals for myself has been a fantastic way for me to create my life, my way.

Here is how it works:

Either by yourself or with your significant other/friend, find a couple of big pieces of paper–a paper grocery bag can work well. You may want to tape some paper together to make the surface bigger. Kristen and I use a 4' x 14' piece of paper when we go through this process.

Step One

In the center of the paper write/draw "Creating My Life, My Way, Today!" If you are working with another person, have them do the same on a separate piece of paper.

Step Two

Randomly write/draw words that categorize your life activities and actions. Make sure to allow plenty of space so you can add additional details around each of your categories. Here are some examples of categories that I like to use:

Family/Friends	Home Environment	Finance
Career/Business	Community	Fun/Recreation
Health/Physical	Personal Growth	

Step Three

After you have developed your categories, focus your energy and attention on each category, one at a time. Write down your ideal goals and outcomes for that category in the coming year. Take your time, writing as many aspirations as you can think of. The key is not to over think your ideas. Usually the first thoughts you think of are what you truly desire. Use the same process for the remaining categories.

Step Four

Compare your Life Creating Visual with your significant other or good friend. Have each person share their entire visual one at a time. Next, start looking for the areas where you can support one another in achieving each other's goals for the coming year. Make sure to talk about the challenges and success factors to achieving the goals and outcomes. Stay realistic, setting yourself up for success instead of failure.

Step Five

When you have your Life Creating Visual completed post it in a place where you can see it every day: the wall into the bathroom, your bedroom mirror, or in the kitchen. Just post it!

I know what some of you are thinking right now, "This is going to be a lot of hard work and take up a bunch of my time." I feel the same way at times and I just don't want to go through the hassle to do this kind of personal growth work. Guess what? I still do it, and then after all is said and done, I wonder why I even hesitated at all. Getting over the hump to create the life you want takes effort. In the end, nothing could be greater than living the life you create each and every day.

Time is running out! How are you going to create the rest of your life?

Get a Goal

Franklin is one of my great mentors. His wisdom continues to teach me because it is as true now as it was in his time. Whenever I am in need of a little inspiration, I visit a couple Franklin Websites that I have bookmarked or I will read pages from his autobiography. Franklin's insights inspire me to think in new ways, which enable me to uncover hidden opportunities and directions.

> *"A man without a goal is like shooting a gun without a target."*
>
> *–Benjamin Franklin–*

When it comes to goal setting, I have always envied people who have been able to set their goals in life at an early age. Rachel Jones, an amazingly brilliant young woman from Zena, knew from early grade school she wanted to be a forensic scientist. Amazing! She focused her energy without ever taking her eyes off the ball, achieving the goal and then working to excel in her profession. This has not been the way life worked for me at all.

How many of you out there are still not quite sure what you want to be when you grow up?

Growing up I wanted to be a paleontologist, or an advertising executive, maybe a formula racecar driver. No, I know, a great author. Or, maybe an influential artist. Could I be the President of the United States? I continue to aspire to very lofty visions. These visions allow me to set my goals and direction in life. Without a strong vision, goals are more like shooting at a target with a shotgun than a rifle.

I have been setting goals tied to my vision for over half my life now. Kristen and I have continued our tradition of collaborating on each other's goals for each New Year. We break down these goals into manageable chunks so we can achieve them. The funny thing is that when you review these goals over the years you will find that we have had way more goals not achieved than achieved, goals that when compared to my 2005 goals would not make our goal chart each year.

We have not been wasting our time on goals that would never be achieved or realized. Quite the opposite. By going after these goals, even if only for a short time, new experiences emerged which enabled me to learn. New doors to possibility have been opened resulting in goals being changed to align with my evolving life vision.

What is holding you back from living your vision and setting your life goals?

> *"Goals: There is no telling what you can do when you get inspired by them. There is no telling what you can do when you believe in them. There is no telling what will happen when you act upon them."*
> *–Jim Rohn–*

Put your goals in writing. If you can't put it on a sheet of paper, you probably can't do what it takes to achieve the goal.

Here is a good starting point for you to set SMART goals.

Specific – stating precisely what is wanted

Measurable – achievement of the goal can be measured

Attainable – you can accomplish the goal; success is possible

Related to Vision – the goal is aligned with your life vision

Time Bound – the goal has a specific date by when it will be accomplished

Setting SMART goals elevates and supports your vision for your life. Start Kicking butt with your life.

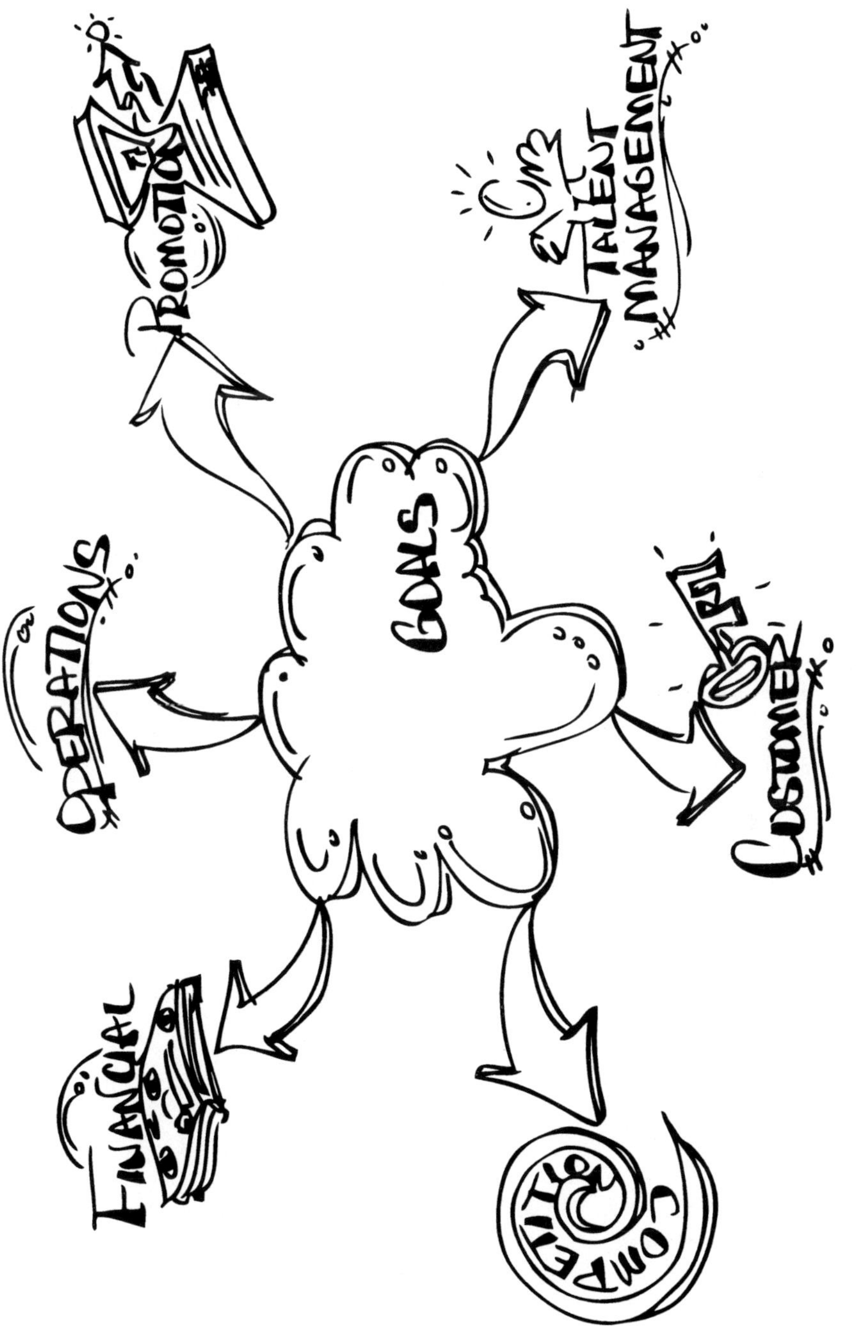
GOALS
PROMOTION
TALENT MANAGEMENT
OPERATIONS
CUSTOMER
FINANCIAL
COMPETITION

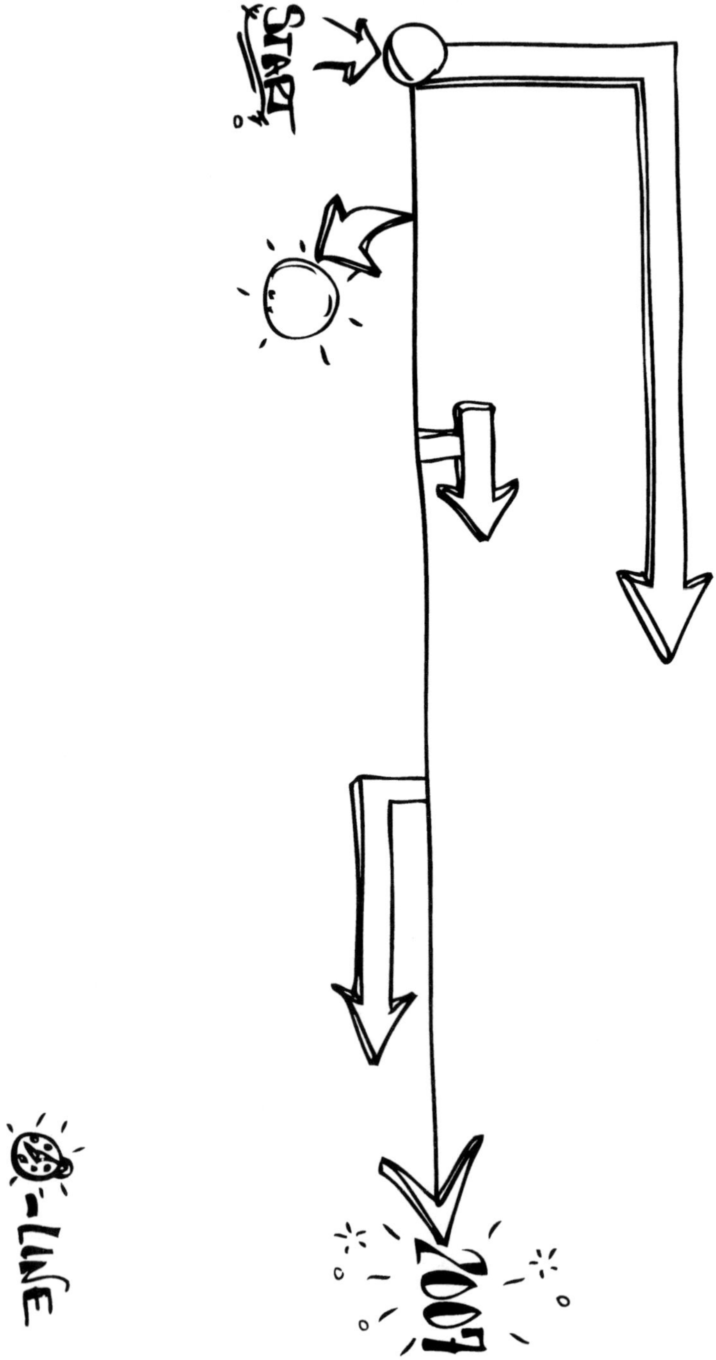
START
2007
-LINE

What Do I Want?

In 2004, I had the surreal experience of being poisoned by the bite of a brown recluse spider. I'm not sure when or where it happened. Other than my flu-like symptoms, I didn't even know that I was poisoned, that is until the skin around the bite started to die. Not so pretty. Being a very active person, maybe you can relate to this, it is not often I carve out any quality downtime to rest and rejuvenate myself, even when I am sick. But relaxing, sleeping, and in general letting my mind wander is what I found myself doing. The influence of the spider bite had my body and mind telling me to rest.

It was in those downtimes, when I was half awake sitting up in my bed, that I did what I do whenever I get some time to rejuvenate myself. I grab one of my sketchbooks and start to visualize what ever comes to my head, in a kind of free flow of consciousness. While I was sketching I started thinking about something I think about quite a bit. That is, "What do I want?" My wants and personal needs have changed over time and I am always re-evaluating what it is that I want so that I can more clearly understand the decisions I have to make to get me where I want to go.

At times I really am not totally sure of what I want. It is during those times that I turn to my personal mission statement which states, "to make a positive difference and show what is possible." My mission statement acts as my ship's rudder and is a reminder of the focused decisions I must make to achieve the vision I have for myself. If "what I want" fits within my mission statement, I am moving in the right direction. *What Box?* is a perfect example of fulfilling my mission statement and achieving that which I have wanted for quite some time: the creation of an interactive forum to share the creativity, joy, hardships, and opportunities held within life lessons and teachings.

This got me thinking on an even deeper level. With so many possibilities within each one of us, how often do we deliberately ask ourselves, "What do I want?" Our uniquely personal wants are as diverse as the situations in which we find ourselves. Yet, in the time you have been alive on this earth, how many times have you deliberately asked yourself, "What do I want?"

"The first step is to find out what you love – and don't be practical about it. The second step is to start doing what you love immediately, in any small way possible."

–Barbara Sher–

Each of our lives is filled with so many choices. If you are going to live the life you want, it is critical to know what it is you want so you can make the choices that will take you there.

Can you name what you want in your life? Most of us have never taken the time to really think about what it is we want or we don't even know how to figure it out.

Here is the part that scares me the most. If you don't make the choices in your life, others will make them for you. Often our choices are a direct result of our circumstances: family, parents, where we grew up, or even our place of birth. Deciding what you want in life is not always easy. This takes practice and patience. When you realize you have the power to make the choices to achieve what it is you want in life a new chapter opens for you, a chapter filled with endless opportunities and possibilities.

Methods to Discover What You Want:

Here are some of the methods I use to discover "What I want" along with what actions to take.

Step 1

Write the title, "What Do I Want?" at the top or center of a blank piece of paper. Then draw or list all the things you want as fast as you can. Just let what you want flow out of you without judgment. Keep on working at it until you have filled as much of the page as possible.

Step 2

Prioritize your wants and develop an action plan. Set goals to achieve what it is you want. Set your goals in 1 week, 1 month, and 6 month increments. When it is really important to me I like to take these written goals and post them where I'll see them daily as a reminder and benchmark to follow.

Step 3

Take the time for a week and keep track of how you spend your time each day. See how much time you focus on attaining what it is you want. At the end of the week evaluate how you spend your time and adjust to focus more on what it is you want.

Step 4

Start capturing ideas you have about your personal vision, mission, and purpose as they come up for you. Save these ideas in a file and keep reviewing and adding to them.

How much time and energy this kind of process takes totally depends upon you. Where you are today is the best place to start. You have everything you need inside of you to take you where you want to go.

Life is so much more rewarding when you are going for and achieving what it is you want from life. The choice is yours.

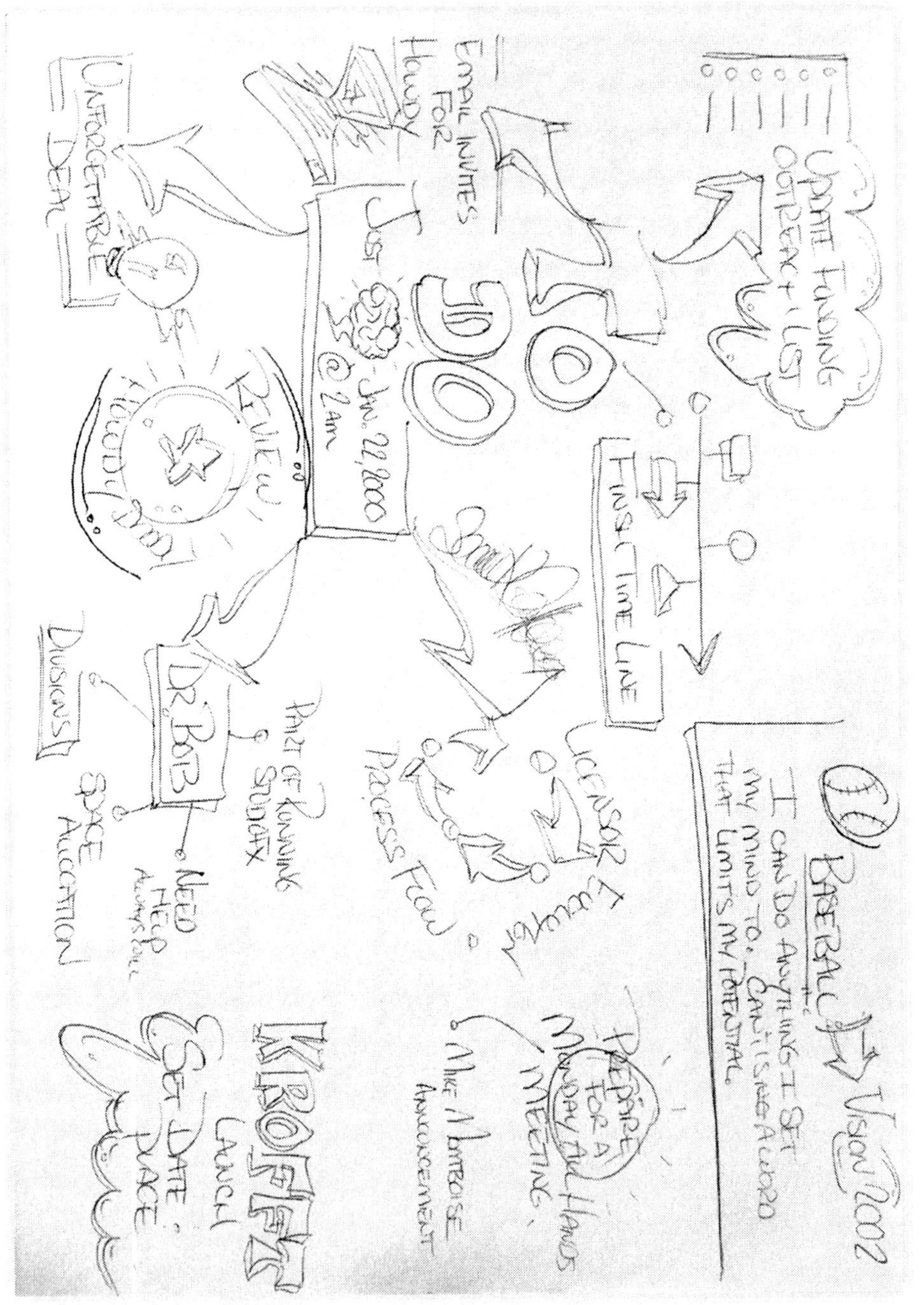
Baseball
Vision 2002
I can do anything I set my mind to. Can't is not a word that limits my potential
Prepare for a Monday All Hands Meeting
Update Funding Outreach List
First Time Line
Process Flow
Email Invites for Holiday
Unforgettable Deal
Dr. Bob
Divisions
Space Allocation
Need Help
Set Date: Place

Remembering Those Who Served

Memorial Day always reminds me of my Grandfather. He served in the army during WWII. I only heard bits and pieces of his time overseas fighting in the war though family members, mostly, during side conversations.

My Grandfather would never talk about his experiences. One time in Irvine, California, I was helping him reinstall a Model A engine in his favorite 2 door. Having so much extra time together my curiosity started tugging on me. After thinking about it for some time, I somehow mustered up the courage to ask him if he had any stories he would like to share with me about his experiences during WWII. Now, my Grandfather was quite possibly the gentlest man I have ever spent time with and I could tell he was more than a little uncomfortable with this question.

He rolled himself out from under the Model A where he was tightening transmission bolts and asked me to sit down on the running board. Boy, I was a nervous and excited at the same time. Then he said, "Son, my experiences during those times are locked away forever. I would not wish the terror and destruction of war on anyone, especially you. Let's not talk about this again." Somewhat in a daze I mumbled that I agreed to his request. And just as quickly as he had sat me down on the running board he was back under the Model A directing me on the reinstallation of the engine.

Like so many other WWII veterans, my Grandfather is dancing with the angels these days and I miss hanging out with him. He was one of my greatest teachers. To this day my Grandfather continues to influence me. What I came to understand after his death as I reflected upon his life was that his experiences of war lead him to place extraordinary value on his quality of life, living each moment to its fullest. This understanding inspired Kristen and me to expand our thinking of what it means to live each moment to its fullest. With this expanded awareness we were able to open up to the possibility of living somewhere besides California, only,who could have imagined it would be in Oklahoma?

I will always hold the service and sacrifice my Grandfather gave to our country with great pride. We are so blessed to live in America and have a home on Grand Lake, one of the most extraordinary places on the planet. With the current War on Terrorism taking our soldiers into new and unforeseen horrors, it is impossible to fully express the gratitude that we all feel on Memorial Day and each and every day of the year. Their lives are being put on the line in much the same way my Grandfather put his life on the line during WWII.

What stories will these new soldiers lock up?

While searching for a powerful Memorial Day quote, I found this very significant statement made by General Douglas MacArthur at the end of World War II, in his speech accepting the Japanese surrender in Tokyo Harbor:

"Men since the beginning of time have sought peace. Various methods through the ages have attempted to devise an international process to prevent or settle disputes between nations. From the very start, workable methods were found insofar as individual citizens were concerned, but the mechanics of an instrumentality of larger international scope have never been successful. Military alliances, balances of power, leagues of nations all in turn failed, leaving the only path to be by way of the crucible of war. The utter destructiveness of war now blots out this alternative. We have had our last chance. If we do not now devise some greater and more equitable system, Armageddon will be at our door. The problem basically is theological and involves a spiritual recrudescence and improvement of human character that will synchronize with our almost matchless advance in science, art, literature and all material and cultural development of the last two thousand years. It must be of the spirit if we are to save the flesh."

When you celebrate Memorial Day, take the time to remember those that have served our country and have made the ultimate sacrifice. Perhaps you can take a moment of silence together or make a toast to all of those who have played such a major role in sustaining America's freedoms so that we can enjoy them.

As my good friend Bart Montgomery would say, "Peace."

Just For Today

JUST FOR TODAY I will live through the next 12 hours and not tackle my whole life problem at once.

JUST FOR TODAY I will improve my mind. I will learn something useful. I will read something that requires effort, thought and concentration.

JUST FOR TODAY I will be agreeable. I will look my best, speak in a well modulated voice, be courageous and considerate.

JUST FOR TODAY I will not find fault with friend, relative or colleague. I will not try to change or improve anyone but myself.

JUST FOR TODAY I will have a mission. I might not follow it exactly, but I will have it. I will save myself from two enemies–hurry and indecision.

JUST FOR TODAY I will exercise my character in three ways. I will do a good turn and keep it a secret. If anyone finds out, it won't count.

JUST FOR TODAY I will do two things I don't want to do, just for exercise.

JUST FOR TODAY I will be unafraid. Especially will I be unafraid to enjoy what is beautiful and believe that as I give to the world, the world will give to me.

SOME KEYS TO SUCCESS
FOLLOW PASSION
HAVE FUN
WALK
RUN
STRIDE
FOCUS
NEVER EVER GIVE UP
FOLLOW INSTINCTS
STAY POSITIVE
BE PATIENT
LET GO
THE PAST
THE FUTURE
EACH DAY
NEGATIVE PEOPLE
MISTAKES
FEAR (FACE IT)
SURROUND YOURSELF WITH EAGLES
LEADERS
AUTHORS
FRIENDS
ASSOCIATES
LISTEN
LIFE LONG LEARNING
READ
EXPERIMENT
NET
CONTINUE ED
GOOD TV
CONTINUOUS IMPROVEMENT
RELATIONSHIPS
FIRST IMPRESSIONS
PERSONAL BEST
TIME USE
FOLLOWING PASSION
FOCUSING
LISTEN
1 MOUTH 2 EARS
ASK FOLLOW UP ?'S
BE PRESENT
SUSPEND JUDGEMENT
VISUAL THINKING
© SEAN GRIFFIN 2001-2004

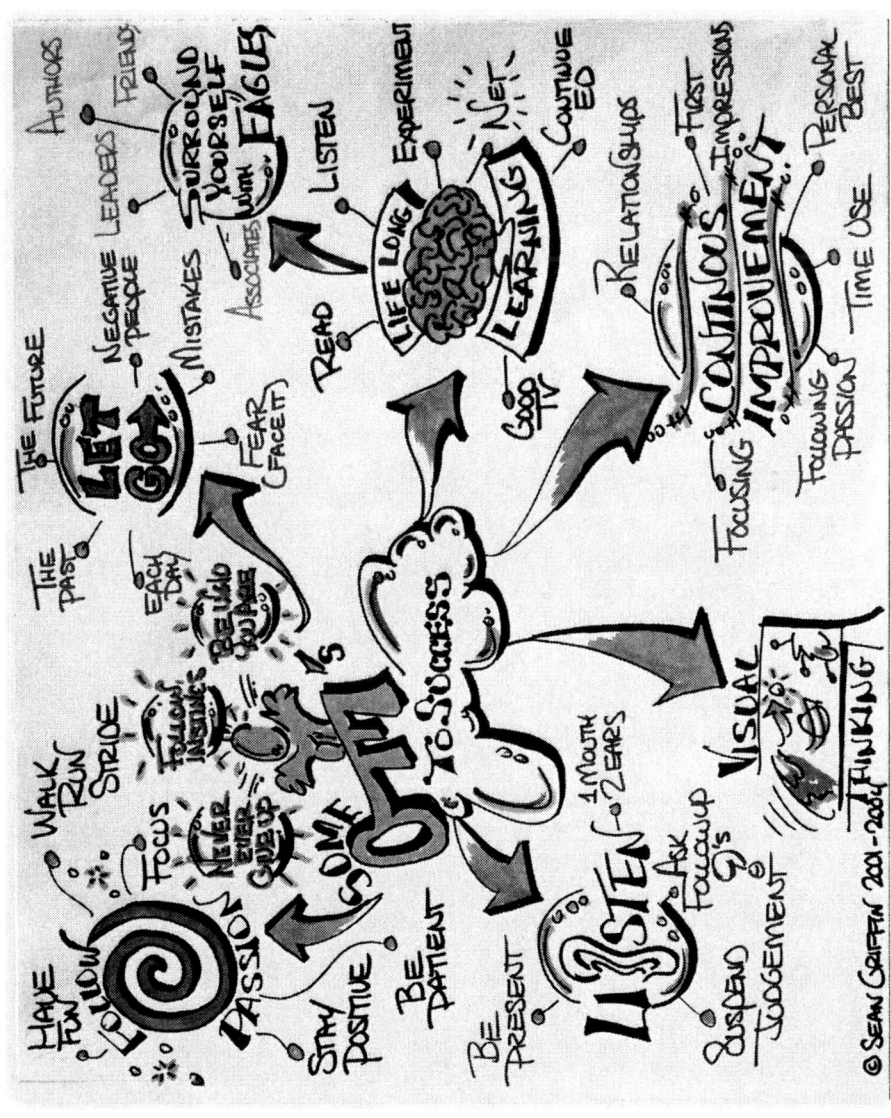

The Courage
To Be
Creative

"The cynic says, 'Only one man can do anything.' One man interacting creatively with others can move the world."

–John Gardner–

The Creative Nature of People

Whle I was watching a little quality TV on Oklahoma Public Television. This particular special was focused on a group of people who were reliving their childhood by taking a train ride along the Colorado River. What they all had in common was that they had all taken, at one time or another, the same train with their family and friends before planes became the new standard for long distance travel.

The train snaked from Denver to Utah and through some of the most challenging and awe inspiring landscape in the United States. The power of the river and beauty of the canyon walls took my breath away even through I was experiencing their adventure on a small screen television.

The wonder, vision and determination to build a train track system through this part of the country got me thinking. It was not that long ago that the only way to get through this treacherous terrain was by horse and even more challenging covered wagon. If you survived the trip it would take you months to reach your destination. 1890 was only 115 years ago. Heck, the Guinness Book of World Records just named the oldest living woman on earth at 125 years old. She was born in 1880. Just think about the change and progress she has been witness to in her lifetime.

What drives all this creative use of energy and imagination?

> *"If necessity is the mother of invention, discontent is the father of progress."*
>
> *–David Rockefeller–*

Creative thinking is the process that humanity has used from the beginning of time. Even the caveman had to be creative in how they controlled fire and in the tools they created to hunt and cook with. As we have learned to expand our creative thinking time has brought us to the modern conveniences that we have today. The types and number of inventions running through the United States patent office is staggering: inventions such as the telephone, fax machines, electric utility companies, planes, hula hoops, railroad systems, personal computers, the pet rock, radio, bifocals, and the television.

The products and services that have emerged from all this creativity and imagination all have one thing in common. They all fulfilled a need and met it head on.

We all have a highly creative and imaginative side. Everyday we see needs to be filled. The difference is in the doing verses the thinking. We all have used what we've had at hand to create something that would serve our purpose. Children have an innate ability to adapt their surroundings to meet their needs. Using their imaginations they create secret hiding places for themselves utilizing what is in their surroundings such as card tables or blankets instead of buying a fort or a tunnel at the store.

When you think about it for a minute you realize that being inventive, using your imaginative and creative side is in our nature. It is how we survive in the world. What a gift!

Alice Fenton is always trying to find ways to use what is at hand without going out to find it elsewhere. I can remember when we were starting a digital multi-media center called the Digital Clubhouse Network, http://www.digiclub.org Alice would go and dumpster dive in high tech company trash bins looking for discarded binders, folders, etc. instead of buying them, which, we couldn't afford to purchase but needed desperately. Thanks, Alice. We couldn't have done it without your persistence to come up with creative and inventive ways to fulfill our needs.

The next time you need something, think up a new idea that fills your need. Do more than think about it. Go out and create it, own it, share it with the world. Your inventive and creative nature has the potential to change the world.

Go for it!

Getting Your Creative Juices Flowing

Whenever I am preparing myself to start writing a *What Box?* story I have to engage in the process of getting my creative juices flowing. Sometimes this is effortless and the words and ideas flow naturally. Other times it can be like pulling teeth and nothing seems to flow at all. This can be very frustrating.

So what can we do to increase the flow of our creative juices when we are blocked and need a jolt of inspiration? Here are few methods I use to get my creative juices flowing.

Finding Balance

When we are always doing, planning, and creating we are not allowing the natural process of our bodies and minds to flow with ease. We need to make time to relax our minds and bodies to be quiet and do nothing, and if at all possible, think about nothing. No small task that is for sure. Our society has us on the treadmill of life and it tends to speed up each and every year. We have to remember that our mind is a living organism that needs breaks. Our mind works in 90 minute cycles. Give it a rest. People who find the time to let their mind wander and relax are able to get their creative juices flowing more effectively than those who continue to burn theirs out.

Walk in Nature

One of the most powerful ways I have found to expand my creative thinking and to get the creative juices flowing is to take a walk in the woods. Nothing seems to open the mind and senses like a good walk outside. It is strange to think that many people go through each and every day only getting outside when they walk from their home to their car or from their job to their car. Living and working on or near Grand Lake is one of the greatest blessings anyone can have. Take advantage of the nature that's around you and get outside and see where your creative juices take you.

"Climb the mountains and get their good tidings. Nature's peace will flow into you as sunshine flows into trees. The winds will blow their freshness into you and your cares will drop off like the falling leaves."

–John Muir–

Let it Go

If you are stuck on something you are trying to figure out and cannot get anything going, walk away from it. Take a break or do something totally different. One of the great secrets of creative genius is to let it go, noodle it, sleep on it, and let the natural process of creativity work for you. The more intent we become on making something happen the more we block inspiration from coming to us. I always like to plan an extra couple of days whenever I have a creative deadline looming. This allows me to work on it a little each day and reflect upon what has been created. In the end the more time I let go and then come back to the creative work at hand the better the end product. Go ahead, give it a try and let it go for a day.

"If you are seeking creative ideas, go out walking. Angels whisper to a man when he goes for a walk."

–Raymond Inman–

Search the Net

In the old days I used to have four library cards that I would use on a regular basis, searching through all the reference material that I could get my hands on. This process allowed me to explore just about anything remaining open for the creative inspiration to hit. Today we have the Internet which provides us with access to unlimited resources to explore any subject you can think of. If you don't have access to the Internet go to your local library or a book store and pick up a bunch of magazines and books. Sit down and start turning the pages, being open to what every creative inspiration comes to you. Don't rush it, take your time, and let the natural flow of creativity run through you. You never know what is possible until you give yourself time to let creativity happen.

Draw it Out of Yourself

Drawing out my ideas is one of the single most important creativity tools I have been able to develop over the years. I literally have over a hundred sketch books with ideas and concepts represented visually. We have all heard it said that some of the best ideas where drawn on napkins. I have been in my share of napkin meetings and I know that many of you have as well. There is a reason for this. What is the reason? Drawing expands your thinking and allows you to let the natural flow of creativity run through your body and mind. More and more I see people with sketch books writing down their ideas. When you draw on hand-made paper the creativity is only intensified. Get yourself a sketch book and start drawing out your best ideas.

Sleep

In my life I have been frustrated, depressed, tuckered out and have felt hopelessness. In these cases I have learned if it is this bad just go ahead and call it a day. Go to bed and sleep it off. Yes, even if it is 1:00 in the afternoon just go ahead and sleep. It is amazing what can happen when you wake up from sleeping off your frustrations. Draw out your first thoughts when you wake up. What were you dreaming about? Taking the time to take care of yourself and sleeping is one of the best ways to recharge your batteries. Go ahead. Give yourself permission to hit that pillow.

Day Dream

I am a big day dreamer. In my life I have day dreamed more than a few days away and what a great use of my time. The time I have on Grand Lake allows me the flexibility to take the time to daydream quite a bit. When you take the time to day dream new creative ideas and solutions arise. Daydreaming may be one of the best ways to get your creative juices flowing. Even if you take 10 minutes to just daydream, to let your mind wander, and then apply those new insights to life, amazing things begin to happen. Go ahead, daydream a day away. "Nothing happens unless first a dream." Carl Sandburg

These are just a few ideas on how to get your creative juices flowing. I use them and you can too. What ways are using to get your creative juices flowing?

Using Creativity to Break Out-of-The-Box

Do you have a desire to increase your creative skills and talents?

More and more of us are being defined by the limiting parameters we set for ourselves, what is commonly known as "a box." People have them, communities have them, corporations have them, governments have them, and animals have them. Our challenge as humans is to figure out how to "break out-of-the-box" that supports creating the limitations in our lives, the box that holds us back as individuals, communities and countries.

If we sit back for a few seconds and think about the idea of a box, we might see that some of the greatest discoveries in history have been uncovered by individuals willing to take a risk and think outside-the-box. Edison's electric light bulb, Walt's Disneyland, Bugsey's Las Vegas, and American's revolutionists are but a sampling of individuals and groups who have changed history by thinking out-of-the-box. Just by saying "I really need to think outside-the-box" we acknowledge that a box exists in the first place.

Creativity comes in all forms. We can think creatively, solve problems, collaborate with people, or invent new tools to make our lives better. We can express ourselves creatively: writing, acting, and teaching, along with drawing and illustrating our ideas. We can dream big dreams like commercial travel in space, mining minerals on the moon, peace on earth for all, or talking with dolphins. Or creativity can be as simple as creating a beautiful space in your garden or knitting a scarf.

Kristen's great creativity comes from her cooking. We all have the creative gene. The question is how can we expand upon it?

Creativity comes when we view any given situation with a fresh and different perspective, thinking outside the box. One of the greatest keys for us to more fully access and utilize our creative potential is to have a positive and open attitude. When we lock ourselves into old and non-productive paradigms we box ourselves in. The challenge is to discover the key that will open the door to support you so that you can consciously exercise your creative muscles and think out-side-the-box on a more consistent basis.

Your creativity is such a wonderful gift. When you begin to act on your creativity what you find inside may very likely be more valuable than what you showcase and share with the external world. You have everything you need to be all you can be.

Where do you want to go?

Reaching Your Creative Potential

Imagine having an endless supply of great ideas at your fingertips. Imagine reaching for your greatest aspirations. Imagine becoming all you want to be.

It takes courage to push ourselves to a place where we have never gone before, to test our limits and to break through the barriers that hold us back. Think about the lion in the 1939 classic film "The Wizard of OZ." The lion, desperately seeking the courage to face life's challenges, is constantly looking outside himself for courage. In all actuality, the lion had an unlimited reservoir of courage already there only he was unable to see that truth about himself.

Just like the lion, we have everything we need inside of ourselves to become all we can be. As Mike Munn, my good friend and former head physicist for Lockheed says, "You know more than you know you know." I would add, "and can be anything you want to be." The challenge for us is to look inward for our strength to stretch and grow creatively instead of looking to the outside world for that strength. Too many times we are held back because we buy into negative outside influences that don't encourage or support different thinking, creative ideas, inventions, or solutions.

In my life I have experienced many fears about being a writer. Growing up, I was challenged by traditional learning institutions. This challenge was compounded by my dyslexia. Writing for me has been torturous at best. As a CEO, my Board insisted that I take writing courses to improve my skills because they were concerned that my "unique" style would not be embraced by the corporate world. For the past 10 years I have been visually representing my ideas about a series of creativity books I want to create and yet, until now, I have not been able to put down more than one paragraph to start the darn thing.

Writing *"What Box?"* has enabled me to embrace the unknown and find the courage to become a writer. What area of your life is holding you back from what you want to do or want to be? What is it that you not doing that you would like to be doing? What do you want to create for yourself?

When we find the courage to go where we have never been before it does not mean that all of the sudden insecurity, fear and anxiety do not exist. Instead we consciously make the decision to move through these feelings as constructively and creatively as we possibly can.

By taking leaps of faith and stepping over the edge into the unknown we stretch our visible and hidden skills to new limits and promote exercising our creative potential.

So the next time you find yourself saying, "Oh, I can't do that," or "That idea is way to over the top," take time and remind yourself that, "Hey, I know more than I know I know and can do anything I decide to do." Believe in yourself and in your abilities and you can accomplish great things.

> *"You see things, and you say 'Why?' But I dream things that never were and I say 'Why not?'"*
>
> *–George Bernard Shaw –*

Tools for Exercising Your Creativity Muscles

Sketch and Doodle Your Thinking

One of the single greatest ways I have found to generate new ideas is to pick up a pencil or pen and start doodling my thoughts. This does not mean you have to possess exceptional drawing skills to draw out your ideas. Stick figures along with simple images have an amazing power to jog your brain consciously and subconsciously, supporting you to reach your goals. These doodles are for your eyes only if you choose. Let go of judgment about artistic merit and instead think of your doodles as a tool to generate new and winning ideas. We have all heard about the idea that was drawn on a napkin and became the next big thing. What idea do you have to draw out of yourself?

Take A Risk

When you are not failing every now and again you are at risk of stagnating yourself and your creativity. When you take a chance you exercise your creativity muscles and continue to strengthen them. Stop doing new things and you loose the creative muscles of risk. Go ahead, take a risk and find something new to do and see where it takes you.

No More Excuses

We have all heard the saying "Just do it!" Sounds so simple doesn't it? When I started writing *"What Box?"* I had to give up on all the excuses that were keeping me from reaching and fulfilling my aspirations. In many cases it takes even more creativity to remove the excuses that hold us back than it does to develop the idea in the first place. What excuses are you holding onto? How can you remove these excuses and become the creative person you were meant to be?

The Subconscious Accelerator

Whenever you are overwhelmed by opportunity or challenges, stare into the diagram to the right for two minutes. It will move, change color, and start supporting the generation of new thinking patterns. It actually changes the wavelengths in your brain to be more in the subconscious.

Once you have completed staring at the diagram for two minutes pick up a pencil or pen and place it in your least dominant hand. If you are right handed use your left hand and if you are left handed use your right hand.

Now make a quick list of your new thoughts and see how they help you to solve problems and think up innovative concepts.

I was first introduced to the "Subconscious Accelerator" by Michael Munn, PhD., former Head Physicist at Lockheed. Thank you, Mike. You are amazing.

You Know More Than You Know You Know

"Ability is what you're capable of doing. Motivation determines what you do. Attitude determines how well you do it."

— Lou Holtz—

What's On Your Mind?

How often do you think about what a phenomenal gift your mind is? Just how phenomenal is it? Your mind thinks and moves energy at the speed of light. Not impressed? Think about it just for a second. Your mind moves energy and ideas at the speed of light. Still not impressed? Let's put it in perspective. In one second, moving at the speed of light you can travel around the world seven and a half times. Now that's impressive! What's even more impressive is that your mind thinks and moves energy at that same speed.

Like computers we only use about 10% of the capacity of our brain. Some of us might push the envelope and use 15% but that is about it. Think of the unlimited potential we are letting sit idle. It is time to stop the brain drain and start using more of our mind's abilities. Each of us has over 1,000,000,000,000 (one trillion) brain cells and a virtual Niagara Falls of bio-chemical information flowing through it.

Yet what do we fill our minds with? In so many cases we fill it with junk. We worry about things that never happen. We over think everything, one of my personal favorites. We think about what we are going to eat. We think about issues of money. We think about trivial facts that don't do much for us at all. We think about the tasks we have ahead of us or, worst all, the things we needed to do but did not get done, which leads us to start stressing out. The list of things we pre-occupy our minds with goes on and on and on and on . . .

In so many cases we don't even know we are doing this because it is such a natural part of our daily, weekly, monthly and yearly thinking activities. When you take the time to slow down, calm the mind, and relax, this is when you can begin to take a look at what your mind is doing. Only then can you start to understand how much of your brain power is being used up by things that really don't matter and, in many cases, are a detriment to your mental and physical health.

Like so many things written about and discussed in *What Box?* this is not easy stuff. If it were easy everyone would be using more of their mind's potential. I have been working on improving my ability to use more of brain consciously for over 15 years now and I am still a long ways away from getting to where I know

I can. The key is to keep on keeping on. Persevere no matter how difficult and you will find yourself becoming more aware of what you are thinking about, what you put into your mind and how you use it. When you program your mind with junk you create junk in your life. If you think you can, you can, if you think you can't, you can't. It is a universal law. This is a small example of how powerful your mind is.

Now you may say, "All right Sean, I am interested in taking a look at what is on my mind. How do I do this?"

One of the first and most important ways is to find a place of silence. I have found nature to be the greatest place to quiet the mind. It is a place to find the inner peace that will allow you see what your mind is doing. Breath slowly, become conscious of what you are thinking about. Let your thoughts flow without judgment. After a while begin to think about what you are thinking about. How does it make you feel? Are they positive thoughts? Are they negative thoughts? Are they thoughts that have nothing do with anything and are a total waste of your brain power? Or are they productive thoughts? Are they thoughts about how to create positive change in your life? Are they thoughts about supporting a better life for yourself and others? Are they thoughts about looking at yourself and how to improve who you are?

The goal is to focus your mind on the productive and positive thoughts. These kinds of thoughts will produce the productive and positive results you desire in your life. It may not happen in a week, it may not happen in a year. It will happen. Behind every overnight success is 20 years of hard work, persistence and positive, productive thinking.

One thing is for sure. The more you practice seeing what is on your mind and using your mind's pathways for productive and positive thought the more efficient your thinking will become and the more positivity will be created in your life. Give it a try. It is never too late to start becoming more aware of yourself. When you do, a whole new world will open to you, a world of unlimited potential and wonder. Go for it. What are you waiting for?

You Know More Than You Know You Know

So how do I really know that I know more than I know I know?

Think of all the experiences you have been exposed to during your life. When you start thinking about these experiences, you begin to realize that you have been exposed to a great wealth of information and knowledge, knowledge you can apply to your individual and community goals and dreams. It is said that today's 18 year old is exposed to more information and knowledge than my Grandfather was exposed to during his entire 78 years on this planet. Wow!

Perhaps one of the differences between those who continue to settle for a life of status quo and those who go on to achieve great things, is that the latter have a willingness and desire to tap into their personal wealth of knowledge. These people have a willingness to stretch themselves and step off into the unknown as a way to increase their learning experiences and base of knowledge.

The brain files away everything we experience or that we are exposed to, yet we only use about 10% of our brain's potential. You lifetime collection of knowledge has tremendous potential to support you in achieving your inner most desires. When you are not using this reservoir of knowledge, it is difficult to move forward, to take risks, and as a result, you hesitate to make the changes that may very well help you get where you want go.

How can you tap into your unlimited wealth of personal knowledge?

In my life, I started to understand that I know more than I know I know while living in California. It happened October 17, 1989 at 4:24pm. I was out mowing the front lawn of my house on a picture perfect tree-lined street in Willow Glen.

Suddenly, the ground under my feet moved. Trees that lined the street began to sway and touch the ground, cars started bouncing across the road, chimneys crumbled in front of me in slow motion. And then, just as suddenly, it all stopped. The moment the movement stopped, it felt as if time stood still for a split second. The Loma Prieta earthquake had hit Northern California. The damage was everywhere.

Just as suddenly, my neighbor across the street, a senior women in her 80's, started running in and out of her house screaming and flailing her arms hysterically. All I could think of doing was to hug her as tight as I could and let her know everything would be alright. After a few minutes of holding her as she cried in my arms, she suggested that she wanted a smoke. On any other day this would have been just fine, but on this day, the whole neighborhood could go up in flames if there were any gas line breaks. For no apparent reason, I stopped her and started smelling the air for gas. To my surprise I could smell the slight hint of gas. I convinced her to not smoke and enrolled another neighbor to stay with her.

Then I went and filled a banana box full of my best bottles of alcohol. This move had the desired calming effect and many neighbors started congregating around the banana box of spirits, listening to the local radio reports and sharing stories.

By this time only a few minutes had passed since the earthquake. That is when the first after shock hit and the smell of gas got stronger. One of my neighbors and I decided to go check everyone's gas pipes and meters. We began knocking on the doors of the remaining residents in the neighborhood, the ones we had not been able to account for. A lady lived in one of the houses on the corner whom I had only seen coming and going in the past. I went up to knock on her door. As I walked up the porch I could hear faint moaning sounds and proceeded to cautiously open the door. There, laying on the floor, was a wonderful, frail, older lady, who was absolutely petrified by what had just happened. This was the first time I had the chance to see the kind of damage that was taking place inside each house. Things were thrown everywhere, pictures where turned upside down, entire china cabinets, contents and all, were smashed on the floor, and the furniture was a jumbled mess.

With the help of a neighbor we were able to slowly get the lady out of her house. We then joined the growing number of neighbors who shared experiences and found comfort in community. I ended up spending the next couple hours going through the neighborhood supporting those that needed support, either emotionally or physically. After PG&E showed up to fix the gas leaks, the aftershocks had become less frequent and the neighbors had a chance to get to know each other a little better, everyone became more comfortable with the situation. It was during this time I was able to slow down and take a breath. While I was winding down, I started to wonder where the heck I had learned such leadership and emergency response skills. Never before had I had to comfort so many people. Never before had I had the opportunity to identify a gas leak and fix it. Never before had I been involved in such a traumatic crisis situation. Yet, I knew what to do without even thinking twice. The energy and flow of that October day is one that I have reflected upon often. That day I put the power of knowing more than I knew I knew into action and ever since, I have been working to do the same each and every day.

What experiences in your life have supported you to be become aware of your understanding that you know more than you know you know? How can you pull that kind of knowing into your life on a more regular basis?

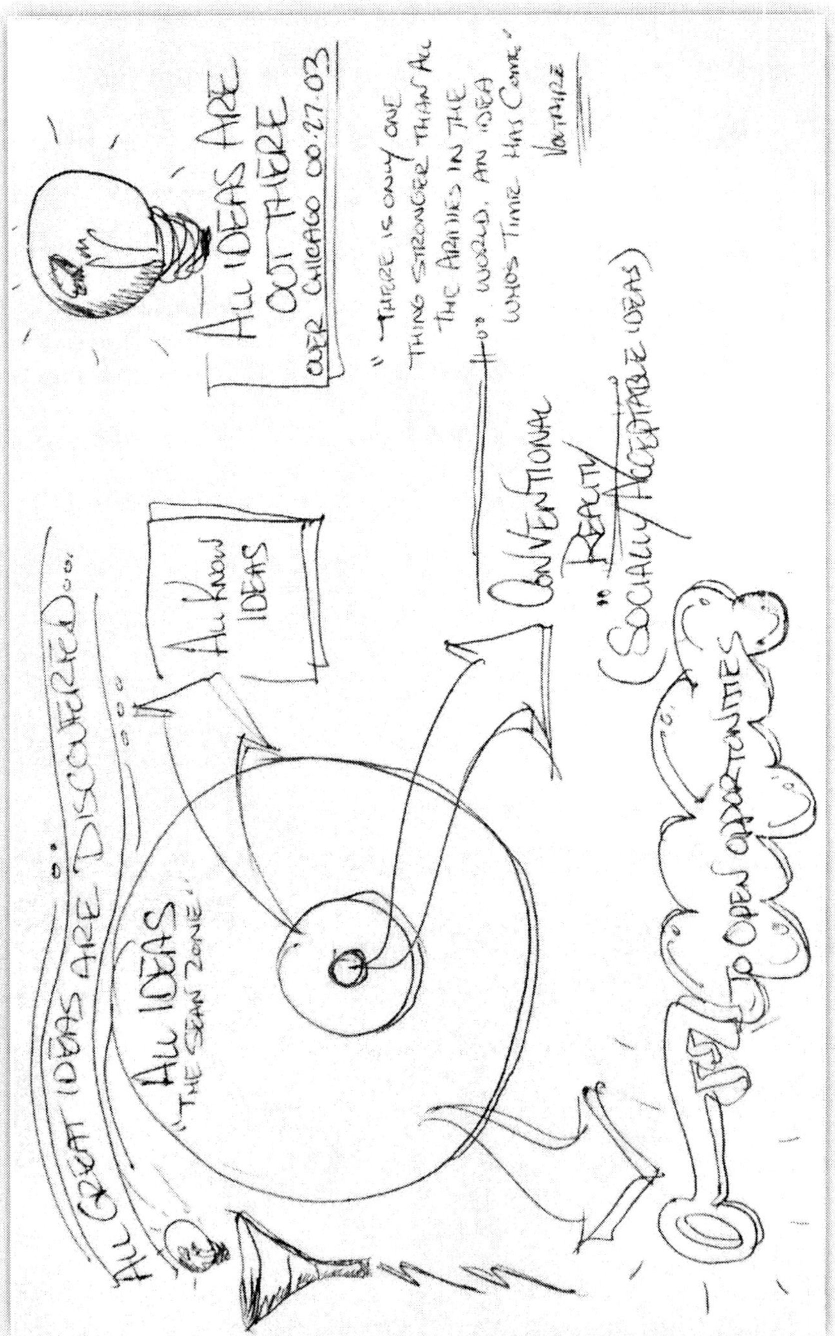
ALL GREAT IDEAS ARE DISCOVERED...
ALL IDEAS
THE SEAN ZONE
ALL KNOW IDEAS
ALL IDEAS ARE OUT THERE
OVER CHICAGO 00.27.03
"THERE IS ONLY ONE THING STRONGER THAN ALL THE ARMIES IN THE WORLD, AN IDEA WHOS TIME HAS COME"
VOLTAIRE
CONVENTIONAL REALITY
(SOCIALLY ACCEPTABLE IDEAS)
OPEN OPPORTUNITIES

Just Suppose

Just suppose you were living life exactly the way you have imagined you want it to be. What does that look like? Are you traveling around the world? Are you swimming with dolphins? Where are you living? What kind of car are you driving? How are you helping the world? Are you taking time to just be? Are you creating that piece of art you have always wanted to create? What kind of career do you have? How are you spending your leisure time?

If you are already living your life exactly the way you have imagined it, congratulations. You are among the select few in the world who have achieved such bliss in life. For the rest of us who continue to dream about a life still not fully achieved there is hope, for each new day has the potential of opening new doors of possibilities. The key is to stay optimistic even through the dark times, the times when our path to living the life we know is possible is shadowed by the daily challenges of living.

It is easy to gain enthusiasm for a dream in the short term. It is a very different thing to remain enthusiastic for that dream through the passing of time. Creating and living the life you want and imagine takes time and hard work. Very few things worth obtaining in life are easy to achieve. This is why so many people fall short, giving up and settling for what is instead of what can be. Don't let this happen to you. You have too much to give back.

When you stay optimistic you are able to see the doors of possibility opening up in front of you. You are able to go through these doors and explore the possibility to see if this new opportunity supports you to live the life you have imagined and are supposed to live. You will start to see your continued perseverance begin to pay off. Each day you make choices that either support your drive to live the life you dream of, or work to hold you back from living that life. We all need to be vigilant to keep the daily stuff that fills our lives from taking over and limiting our ability to see new opportunities.

Just living in today's "super human" environment is enough to drag anyone down. When you let skepticism and pessimism take over your state of being, you derail your efforts to living the life you have imagined. I have met many people who have let the challenges of living take over and suppress them from becoming what they know they can become. They have given up and, worst of all, in many cases only complained about their situations as if they had nothing to do with it. They did and you do too.

Suppose for example, that you will make only the best choices for your life from this point forward. What choices will you make? Who will you choose to hang out with? Who will you choose not to hang out with? What health choices will you make? What will you choose for your life?

I suppose life is a journey of ups and downs, highs and lows. It is how we choose to respond to these highs and lows and ups and downs that allow us to appreciate the highs that much more. Sometimes this may mean taking a day as "a do over day" or perhaps you will just go to bed and look forward to tomorrow and a new day. When you are able to focus on the positive even during the times when your path to living the life you know is possible is shadowed by the daily challenges of living, you are on your way to making the most out of your life and the lives of those around you.

Some Days Are Whackier Than Others

Ever had one of those days where your equilibrium is just out of whack, where things are not going well and you end up communicating or acting in ways you wish you could take back or some how receive a "do over?"

Why is it that some days things just seem to be out of Whack?

Many times we have been upset by something earlier in the day that effects our actions. Perhaps we are overworked and are having a difficult time focusing. I know that when I have large challenges and, particularly, when there is more than one thing coming at me all at once I tend slip into a mindset of overwhelm. This results in my saying and doing things that I regret, things that if I were focused, balanced and present in the moment, would not happen.

Not every day can be a great day, an "on" day. Sometimes the hardest days hold the greatest potential for personal growth. When you say, "Ok, where are the op-portunities to learn from this situation?" you start growing, one day at a time. This is where it takes all of our strength so that we are able to realistically look at our unique situation and uncover those areas where we can improve ourselves and then apply these lessons to our lives. No small task indeed.

> *"Should you shield the canyons from the windstorm,*
> *you would never see the beauty of their carvings."*
> *–Elisabeth Kubler-Ross–*

How can we face the realities of our life and the choices we make?

It is important to show up each and every day, be open to the possibilities that may unfold and take responsibility for our actions. If you have done something that you believe could have been done better or that was a mistake, say, "I'm sorry, I made a mistake and I want to apologize." Sorry seems to be one of the hardest words for people to say today. I wonder why?

Is it because we will be seen to have flaws? Or that people will think we are failures? No matter what it is that holds us back from saying we are sorry or that we made a mistake in the end does not serve us well. We are all humans prone to making mistakes. Everyone makes mistakes. The challenge is to acknowledge our mistakes and learn from them so that we don't make them again. This shows strength, balance, and a truth none of us can run from.

We are all humans and as such we all have faults that at one point or another will rear their ugly heads.

> *"To err is human; to admit it, superhuman."*
> *−Doug Larson−*

When you say, "I'm sorry and I made a mistake," miraculous things happen. The person receiving the apology is grateful, and has a greater trust in you. In addition you have taken one step closer to understanding and facing the realities of your actions. With a sigh of relief you start to learn that it wasn't as bad as you thought it would be. Although difficult, whenever I have made the effort to say, "I am sorry" for something I have done, my relationship with that person has grown stronger. And isn't stronger relationships what we all want?"

What a wonderful place the world would be if we would all acknowledge our mistakes, learn from them and work to keep them from happening again. This is important on many levels: personal, community, town, city, state, nation and the world.

When we wake up each morning we have no way of really knowing how our day is going to go. We do have a choice of how we will respond or act as any given situation comes up. Take a deep breath and know that some days are just whackier than others.

Playing the Game

As children growing up, we all learn how to play with one another through games, all kinds of games. I can remember playing flashlight tag with the other kids in my cul-de-sac. Monopoly was the most popular game with my family on rainy days. Candy Land was another favorite and then there was The Game of Life. I can hear the wheel in the middle of game board spinning right now. Where it lands nobody knows. Growing the biggest family, securing the best career, buying the house on the hill, all while avoiding the pit falls of playing The Game of Life.

If only playing the real game of life was as easy as the board game. How do you play the game of life? Growing up I was never taught how to play the game of life. In fact, I have rebelled against buying into this game and instead created my own rules. I have experienced this game as unhealthy and full of low integrity people serving themselves before others. By creating my own game on the sidelines of the larger game, a kind of ghost in the machine, I have been able to excel with an "out-of-the-box" way of life that has served me well. At least, that is what I have thought. I have been proud to be an example of someone who has not played the game and been able to succeed in life against all odds.

Looking back on my childhood I can see that everything I needed to learn about playing the game could have been learned from my time in the sandbox. We had to share the toys that were available to us. Collaboration was necessary for those in the sandbox to get along and create something. When a bully would take a toy or your sandwich you had to decide to fight or flee. The interactions that took place in the sandbox are a great place to reflect upon how to play the game. What happens between childhood and adulthood is that we forget these lessons?

As I have become more motivated and focused on sharing the power of *What Box?* and have been consciously living it, it has become clear that I not only have to start playing the game, but start embracing playing the game. This is a major challenge. How does one step into the box, yet remain out-of-the-box and keep their sanity? Sounds like one of those wise sage questions that doesn't have an answer doesn't it?

How odd, that to support people, organizations, communities and corporations to think more out-of-the-box you have to step into the box and play the game. This is the way it is and to create a meaningful impact in people's lives it is critical to become a champ at playing the game. I have been in awe and at the same time in contempt of people who can play the game with great ease.

> *"Difficulties are meant to rouse, not discourage. The human spirit is to grow strong by conflict."*
>
> *–William Ellery Channing–*

How can we learn to play the game even better and still remain unique?

I don't even know how to fully enter the game. Is there a starting point? Did I miss it and now am I in the middle somewhere on the game board? How do I catch up? What are the rules and who created them? Is there more than one game? Is there a get out of jail free card? Do I get to pass Go and collect $200?

I believe the challenge is to stay conscious of the fact that we are all playing the game, while staying true to our values and mission in life. It's kind of like standing next to yourself, watching and reminding yourself not to take it too seriously and have fun while playing. Aren't games supposed to be fun?

Like so many things in life and written in *What Box?* it takes tremendous practice to achieve the desired results. I have a feeling this one is going to take the rest of my life to figure out. I guess we all have to figure it out for ourselves.

Playing the game is part of life. We can embrace it or repel it. Which will you choose?

Perfectly Imperfect

The talents displayed by Olympic athletes totally amaze to me. I think this is the main reason I watch the games so intently. The athletes' quest for perfection got me thinking about perfection as a goal. I thought about what my friend Nolan Bushnell, the founder of Atari and Chuck E. Cheese Pizza, said about perfection. He said, "The pursuit of perfection leads to stagnation and then eventually to paralysis." This is something I remind myself of whenever I am getting too perfectionist oriented. I can understand the desire for perfection to be the goal at the Olympics, but in everyday life I think we fall prey to the idea that we have to be perfect in every way . . . and so does everyone else. Aren't we all "perfectly imperfect" just as we are? When we are being the best we can be, is that not also perfection?

If I were a baseball player my batting average would be something like 0.169. I miss more baseballs and strike out way more than I hit the ball, never mind a single, double, or a home run. Kristen is laughing right now because I have used baseball as a metaphor. The only sport I really enjoy is a good Formula car race. The thing is that the baseball metaphor could not be much better. After all, what other activity rewards a person so well for getting it right less than 30% of the time? You have to swing at a lot of balls; we are talking a lot of balls, before you connect with one in a meaningful way.

In my life I have made more mistakes, messed up more situations than I care to remember and, in general, have struck out more than I have connected. I have been depressed and felt tremendous hopelessness in my life as a result of some of these mistakes. The difference is that instead of giving up or developing a pessimistic attitude towards life, I have learned from these mistakes and embraced the opportunities within them. By looking at how I contributed to the mistakes I have uncovered new perspectives on how to move forward with my dreams and aspirations. Each time I just had to find the courage to remind myself that I am "perfectly imperfect" and that everyone makes mistakes.

I can remember one such experience as if it happened yesterday. In 1995 I was starting some of my very first consulting gigs and was hired by the Board of the Lucille Packard Children's Hospital at Stanford University. For this project I was hired to graphically facilitate the Board's yearly strategic planning session. In graphic facilitation I support groups to think more visually by facilitating them through traditional meeting processes while capturing the ideas developed during the meeting visually on a wall. I do this with a hand full of colored markers and a piece of paper approximately four feet wide by twenty feet long. With these simple tools I translate the ideas generated during the meeting into images that are easy to understand. Not only am I drawing pictures representing these complex ideas live and in real time, I am capturing key thoughts in words. This particular Board made up of some of the most prestigious doctors in the world were very focused on my mistakes this particular day.

Being a dyslexic, words are always a bit of a challenge. Even when I know the word and how it is spelled I will simply misspell it. You can only imagine what happens when the words are coming from a doctor's vocabulary. As we all have experienced at one point or another when a doctor is speaking in doctor talk they do not always speak English. As I misspelled the first word the meeting came to a halt because it had to be corrected. I reminded them that, "Hey, this is hand made. Let's focus on the content and not so much the accuracy because we can correct the spelling later." No such luck. As the meeting continued the words got harder and harder and I misspelled more and more often. By the time eight hours had passed I actually had to hold back the tears because some of the Board members were so totally focused on the spelling being correct before we could move forward with the meeting.

When I finally got back home I was thinking, "What am I doing this for? I don't need this torture. Forget this crap." While I was venting and sitting on my bed stewing I picked up the dictionary I always keep close at hand. I started looking up the words I had misspelled and began writing them down. I was thinking, "I will never misspell this word again," and proceeded to write the words I had misspelled in front of all those Board members over and over and over,kind of like the way teachers have kids write on the chalkboard. The process of writing those words gave me confidence and I realized that instead of giving up my work as a graphic facilitator I could write down the words I consistently misspell and learn how to spell them correctly on a regular basis.

After 11 years and graphically facilitating hundreds of meetings I continue to misspell words, only now I have learned how not to be so hard on myself and remind myself that I am "perfectly imperfect." What could be more perfect? What are your experiences with perfection?

If It Were Easy Everyone Would Do It

"Life without risk is not worth living."

–Charles Lindbergh–

Is Your Time Slipping Away?

While attending a Willie Nelson concert I started wondering what he was thinking while on stage singing his classic hit from the early 60's for the umpteenth million time. As a living legend his longevity and popularity is a testament to his powerful ability to sing songs of truth that touch the soul.

> *"Ain't it funny how time slips away?"*   —*Willie Nelson*—

Seems like every time you turn around another year has passed. No wait, was that really ten years ago?

As a youth, whenever I was doing something that my grandparents thought was a waste of time, probably watching another episode of Leave it to Beaver on the boob tube, one of them would surely sit me on their lap and start explaining the following jewel of wisdom, "The older you become the faster time passes by. It serves you better that you work to make the most out of each and every moment, young man." Then we usually would start to garden, to work on one of their Model A's or visit a museum. These words of wisdom and experiences that will live with me forever.

What words of wisdom and experiences of life do you hold on to and embrace?

As I have grown older and wiser, the barnacles on my back are starting to show, in more ways than one. I have begun to realize that the more I know the less I know and that each and every moment is a gift to be cherished. The challenge for me, the challenge for all of us, is to learn how to focus our limited time and energy on those things that positively empower us and those around us.

For a great majority of us it seems as though time is something that there is never enough of. Why do we seem to fill every minute of our day always doing things: driving, meeting, planning, selling, buying, creating, learning, working, flying, interacting, eating, drinking and cleaning only scratch the surface of the examples that exist when we are in the "doing" mode.

Just a few minutes of peace and quiet can help calm the soul and relax the mind, allowing us to open up to new and inspiring thoughts. These are the kinds of thoughts that Willie Nelson probably experienced and embraced while creating many of his timeless songs. Yet, why is it that we tend not to take the time to be still, quiet the mind, and consciously relax, thus allowing us to become more aware of the impact each moment of time that passes has on our lives?

> *"Nothing valuable can be lost by taking time."*
> *–Abraham Lincoln–*

Every time we take a moment to just be is an opportunity to open the doors of perception and gain a greater understanding and awareness of our life choices, responsibilities, decisions and actions. How can we create the space for some peace and quiet in our daily lives? It seems as though we are constantly bombarded with media messaging that tells us we are not good enough, that we aren't doing enough, that we don't have enough stuff and that our stuff is not big enough.

Just so you know, you are perfect the way you are right now. Perfectly imperfect.

Grand Lake O' the Cherokees is one of those extraordinary places on earth that inspires us to slow down, enjoy the moment and cherish the time that we have in our lives. How many of us really take the time to slow it down? You know what I am talking about, watching the birds, reading a book, cooking with family, taking a walk in nature, boating around the lake with no particular place to go, or just sitting in one of your favorite spots consciously participating in the world that is unfolding around us? What places near where you live give you an opportunity to slow down and take in the world around you?

> *"Dost thou love life? Then do not squander time, for that's the stuff life is made of."*
> *–Benjamin Franklin–*

No matter what your age, don't let time slip away from you. It was Colonel Sanders of Kentucky Fried Chicken who started his own company at the tender age of seventy two that now reaches around the globe. This wonderful example of never ever giving up helps to highlight the universal truth of "anything is possible."

Focus on the positive, focus on your passions, focus on making a difference, focus on being the best you can be, focus on living your dreams, and remember to be patient with yourself. I slip up all the time. You'll slip up too. It won't be easy. Heck, if it were easy to live a life of purpose everyone would be doing it. You can do it! Go for it! There is no time like the present to start living your life to its fullest potential.

The Art of Sustainability

Each and every day we make choices, choices that affect our lives and that of others. What we value and how we think of others influences the decisions and choices we make. What do you value and how does this affect your decisions?

Today more than ever it is critical to see the world through a lens of sustainability and equality for all. As a world we are consuming more of the earth's resources than ever before and polluting our world at an ever increasing rate, an unsustainable level. Many seem to take a short view and make decisions based upon what impact they can create in the immediate future without regard for the long-term consequences of these decisions. Our challenge as individuals and as a community is to think about the long-term effects of our decisions, to look out farther than five years and instead think in terms of five generations. No small task indeed.

Living and maintaining a sustainable life does not mean that you have to give up all the joys of life we have become accustomed to and in many cases take for granted each day. Quite the opposite. Living a sustainable life means taking the time to buy foods that are locally grown, clothing that is made from natural or recycled materials, or driving your car just a little less. As an example, Kristen and I belong to two co-ops in Tulsa that provide us with so much food each week that are able to avoid shopping at Wal-Mart, in fact we have not shopped at Wal-Mart in over seven months running.

It has not been easy to reduce our dependency on Wal-Mart. We had to make a conscious effort to shift our thinking and patterns of buying, spend a little extra, and go out of our way to make it work. In the end the benefits are well worth the time and cost. The food we buy is locally grown, organic, and tastes way better than any other we have eaten besides the stuff that comes from our veggie garden in Zena. All the vegetables last at least a week longer than the stuff you buy in the stores and hey, we are supporting the local economy of our farmers. What could be better?

Native Americans have understood the importance of sustainability for generations. Whenever they were looking to make important decisions that would affect the entire tribe they would consider their decision with the perspective of how it would affect future generations. Native Americans were sensitive to how they impacted the areas where they lived, hunted, grew crops, and interacted. They knew when it was time to leave and let the area in which they lived rejuvenate itself by letting nature work her magic. They would scout out a new and abundant place to live for as long as that place could sustain them. We have a lot to learn if we are to sustain our current way of life.

Somewhere along the path we have lost our relationship with our local community and the surroundings of our planet. If we do not gain a better perspective and rethink our relationship with our environment, our local communities, and the planet we call home we are sure to reach a limit that will force us to adjust our lifestyle. We cannot be like the proverbial ostrich and hide our heads in the sand. Wouldn't it be more productive to take a proactive approach to our changing world and think about our decisions from a sustainable point of view? Our children, grandchildren and future generations are all depending on us to make the right choices.

Pursuing practices that will lead to "sustainable livelihood for all" can be such a formidable challenge that to many it seems unrealistic or not worth the effort. Here is the thing. If we are to leave a legacy of lasting positive stewardship for our local communities and the planet for future generations, we must take the steps to change our view of a sustainable community, a long view that includes everyone and everything in the choices that we make. In the end, our individual choices will not only have a sustainable impact on the communities in which we live, but will have an impact on a sustainable world. The choice is yours. What will you choose?

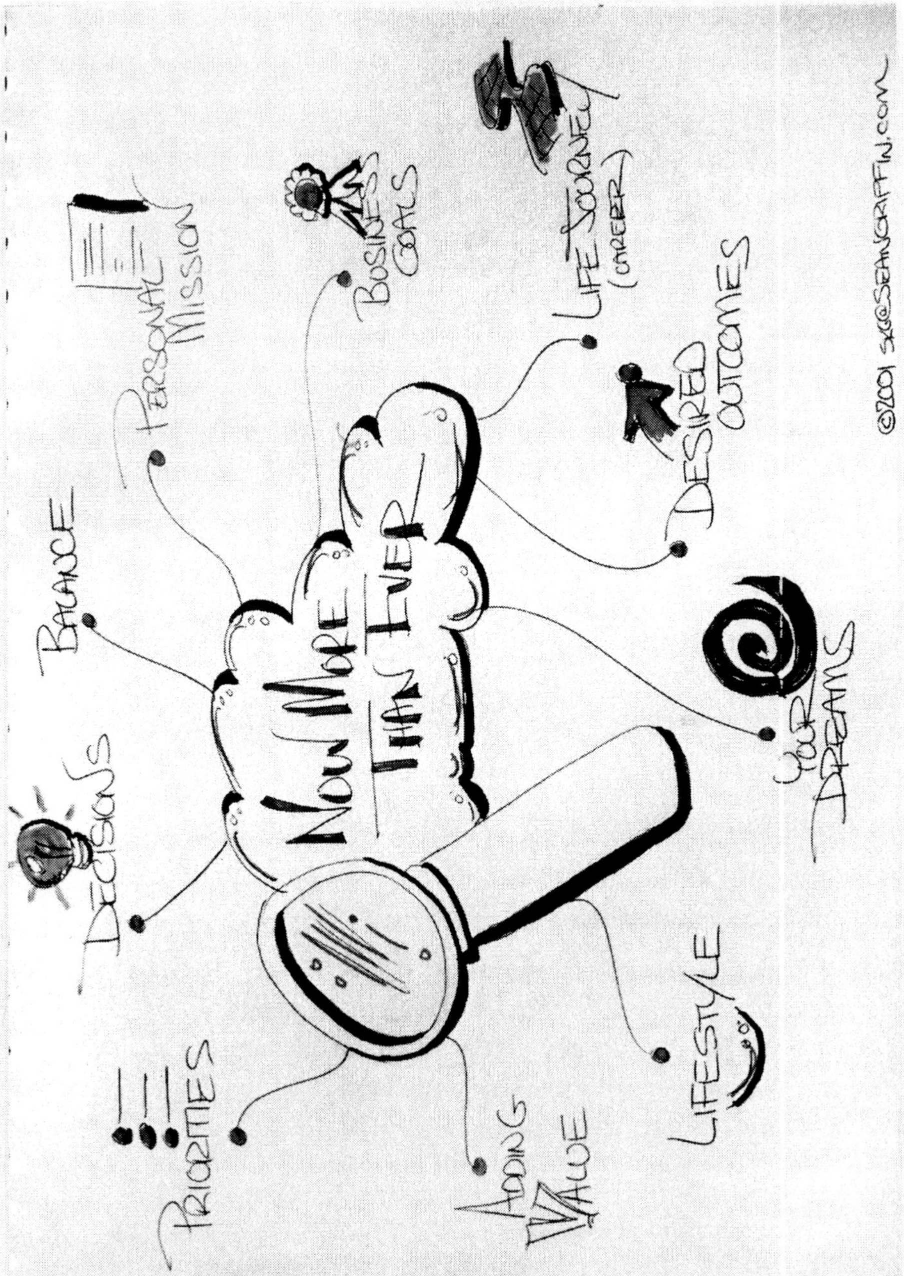
Now More Than Ever
Balance
Personal Mission
Business Goals
Life Journey
(Career)
Desired Outcomes
Your Dreams
Lifestyle
Adding Value
Priorities
Decisions

The Art of Relationships

I frequently sit and think about the next story that I will write for ***What Box?*** I visually represent my ideas and create lists, lots of lists. Some people refer to me as "Sean Penn" because every time they see me I'm illustrating my thoughts in one of my notebooks. Over time this list has grown so much that now I have enough ideas to fill the pages of several books. This particular time nothing inspired me enough to put it down on paper. Writing for me is kind of like creating art. You just never really know when the inspiration to create will hit.

So I decided to let it go for a while, giving myself time to allow for inspiration to take hold.

While I was letting go, I kept thinking about my relationships: relationships from the past, current relationships, new relationships, timeless relationships, life altering relationships, business relationships, imagined relationships, all my relationships. I thought about how fortunate I have been to experience so much love through being in these relationships. I started thinking, "How the heck have I created so many meaningful relationships in my life in such a short period of time?"

The art of building relationships was certainly not learned from classes in school. I mean, why Relationship Building 101 is not a required course taught in school from kindergarten on is not clear to me. There is quite possibly nothing more important in life than the attainment of relationship building skills to support our personal growth and the attainment of our dreams and desires. We all need help and support and the only way I have found to gain that is through building and retaining meaningful relationships.

I believe I learned the art of relationship by being around adults a lot while growing up. When I was not in school I was with my mother working on legislation in support of challenged students. If not with my mother and her cronies, I was with my father at his architectural firm drawing floor plans. Or I was out at social gatherings with my parents interacting with adults, experiencing and talking about adult things. It must have been strange to be one of my parent's friends with their kid always hanging around being engaged and engaging them. Looking back now I realize these experiences accelerated the development of my relationship building skills.

For me the art of relationship is about giving more than it is receiving. When I go for a relationship I am very focused on learning about that person, what motivates them, what their dreams are, and how I can support them in their quest. Sometimes it just means listening. Now as a man this is not always easy, because, like most men, I have a tendency to want to fix things. I always have to remind myself that I have two ears and one mouth and to use them accordingly. Just so you know, I figure it will take the rest of my life to get this one right.

When you give of yourself without the expectation of getting anything back from a relationship you will, in the end, gain more from the relationship. It may sound strange, but when you go after a relationship only looking at what you will gain from it, you lessen the power and rewards of developing a long and meaningful relationship.

So many of us are influenced by society's unrelenting desire to ask, "What have you done for me lately?" Turn this ineffective thinking around and ask, "What can I do for you today?" I bet you will see that your whole world changes for the better and that in return for all you give you will receive that much more. How can you sow the seeds of meaningful relationships? How can you go for the relationship that is about giving instead of taking?

In the end, a long-term meaningful relationship is about both giving and taking. I like to look at it as bank account. The more you withdraw or take from the relationship without depositing, the less confidence, influence and trust you have in the relationship. The more you deposit, give into the relationship, the more confidence, influence, and trust you have in the relationship.

Words

Next to the power of the written word, the spoken word is one of man's greatest gifts. Words give us the power to create. Words can be used to inspire, motivate, empower, hurt, damage, improve, and innovate. When we speak, the words that we use have so much potential and are so powerful that we can positively change our lives and that of others or we can destroy them. And yet, how often do we really think about what it is we are speaking? Is what we are speaking really communicating what we mean? How can we learn to choose words to communicate our thoughts from a place of integrity and truth on a regular basis?

Sometimes people pay a high price for speaking with integrity and are not always popular. Abe Lincoln was an example of a man of great integrity, a man who was faithful to his principles and honest and courageous in expressing his beliefs. Abe's words are second only to the Bible in published books and his words are still recalled today by leaders all over the world as inspiration and motivation for them as they take on the challenges of the future.

Thinking of Abraham Lincoln I am moved by yet another man who gave so much of himself and continues to inspire generations of people all over the world. Martin Luther King, Jr. was a powerful man who was not always popular when he spoke with integrity. We all know, "I have a dream" as the beginning of one of the most memorable speeches in modern history. His words have only grown stronger over time and now memorials are being built in cities all over the world sharing his words. This is the kind of power words have to affect history and change.

What I am wondering is how do we, on a regular basis, say and communicate what we mean, speak from a place of integrity and use the power of our words to create truth and joy in our lives and that of others? How do we block the words that are negatively used against ourselves and that of others? Quite a challenge I must say.

Let's be honest. It's not easy to be aware of the words we speak all the time or even most of the time. At times we are not totally sure of what it is we want to communicate. Other times the limitation of our language gets in the way and it can become too difficult to express ourselves. Yet, other times we are not even thinking about what it is we are saying. Ultimately this is where we get ourselves into trouble. In too many cases people have gone on autopilot and don't even have a clue what they are communicating. We have the power to break out of these autopilot patterns. Like so many concepts and ideas shared in *What Box?* it takes practice, patience, and persistence to achieve the desired goal, in this case, becoming aware of the words you are speaking and then learning to choose words that support communicating from a place of integrity. Practicing these actions will support creating a positive impact in your life and the lives of those around you.

Here are some of the ways I have experimented with to become more in tune with the words that I use:

Listening

Pay attention to words other people use by listening. People like to be around people who listen to them. Listen to the words used most and if the words were positive or negative. See what words draw you in or drive you away. Listen!

Become Aware of the Words You Use

Think about and focus on what you are saying in your daily communications with people and groups. Become aware of the words you use to communicate and identify the words you use the most. With those words think about the meaning of words you would like to be saying. When you start paying attention to the words you use, observe how people respond differently and build on the positive.

Focus on the Positive

We have all heard it before. I can hear my Great, Great, Great Grannie Arant off in the distance, "You gain a lot more with sugar than with vinegar." Focusing on the positive supports creating what you want in your life. People really like to be around positive people. No matter how bad it may seem there is a positive side.

Words to Avoid

Avoid using negative words towards yourself and others. When you express anger, jealousy, envy, or hate you hurt yourself and those around you. Avoid gossiping about others and forming opinions prematurely.

Our ability to express ourselves through words is such a great gift. In the end you decide which words you will choose to best describe what you want to communicate. The words you choose have the power to set you free, or enslave you. By paying more attention to the words that we use and saying what we really mean, we can change ourselves and the world around us for the better. You have the power. What do you have to say?

Living Your Mythical Journey

"Every one of us has in him a continent of un-discovered character. Blessed is he who acts the Columbus of his soul."

–Quoted in Words of Life, edited by Charles L. Wallis–

Living Your Life With Passion

The idea that we own something is really quite strange if you take the time and think about it for just a minute. Because our lives are temporary as such, so are our possessions. You can't take them with you. When we are overly attached to the things that we own or desire to own, we run the risk of identifying ourselves with those things. Things we own and money we accumulate can be lost in a matter of minutes. If we become so attached to things that we loose our own unique self in the process we are setting ourselves up for disappointment and depression. That is because our ownership is temporary just like us. The measure of our greatness is not based upon what we take from the earth but what we leave behind.

There is one thing that you have that is uniquely yours and you will still own no matter what is taken from you or lost. It is the most important thing you have and no one else has it except for you. No one can take it away from you. What is it? It is your passion for life, living your unique life in harmony with all life. This does not mean the drive for day-to-day lusts or the pursuit of self-actions. These will only prove to be short lived and unfulfilling, failing to bring any kind of lasting fulfillment.

Life is a great journey with ups and downs. Part of the process is living your life with passion and joy. Joseph Campbell liked to call it "following your bliss." Here is what he had to say on the subject. "If you follow your bliss, you put yourself on a kind of track that has been there all the while, waiting for you, and the life that you ought to be living is the one you are living. Wherever you are, if you are following your bliss, you are enjoying that refreshment, that life within you, all the time."

Living your life with passion has the ability to release the attachment of self-centered goals and aspirations that only fulfill the needs of your ego or self. Let's face it. This is hard stuff. No one said the journey was easy. It is worth the pursuit because it means you are allowing your true self to arise and that nothing of real importance and value can be taken from you. When you are living your true passion, you become identified with your unique self not things, stuff or the limitations of the physical world.

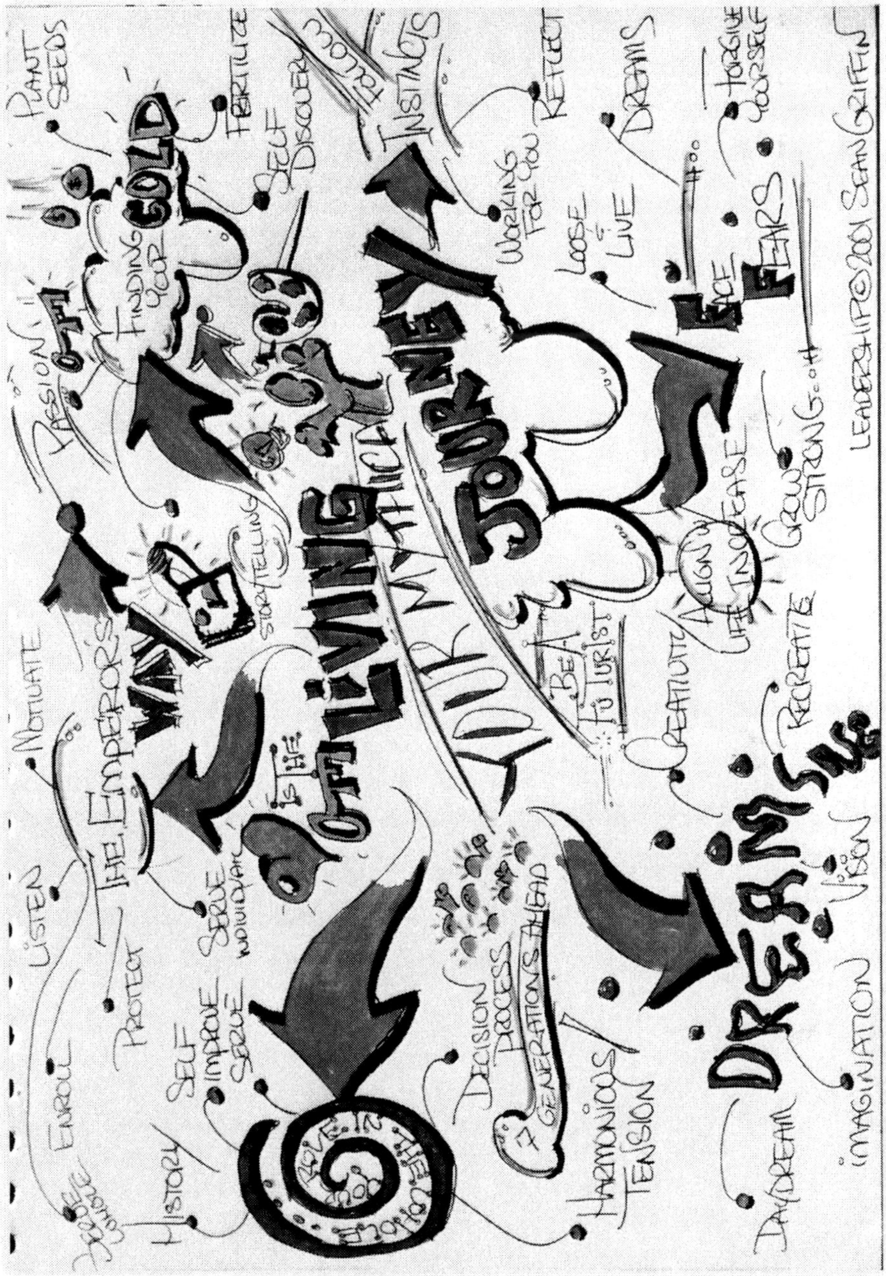
LIVING YOUR MYTHICAL JOURNEY
THE EMPERORS WAY
FINDING GOLD
DREAMS
FACE FEARS
STORYTELLING
DECISION PROCESS
7 GENERATIONS AHEAD
HARMONIOUS TENSION
DAYDREAM
IMAGINATION
VISION
RECREATE
CREATIVITY
BE A FUTURIST
ALLOW LIFE INCREASE
GROW STRONG
FORGIVE YOURSELF
LOOSE LIVE
DREAMS
WORKING FOR YOU
REFLECT
INSTINCTS
SELF DISCOVERY
PLANT SEEDS
FERTILIZE
PASSION
MOTIVATE
LISTEN
PROTECT
SERVE INDIVIDUALS
SELF IMPROVE SERVE
HISTORY
ENROLL
LEADERSHIP©2001 SEAN GRIFFIN

So how do you discover your unique and powerful passion? Each and every moment of your life is an opportunity to uncover and live your unique passion. You will know when you are living your passion because everything will feel right. There will be no hesitation, no second thought. There will be nothing but harmony and bliss. You don't need to do anything but let the harmony and passion flow through you. When you feel this kind of alignment with life, your unique passion, follow it, live it to the fullest and don't stop living it.

When you are living and following your passion, you align with what has been there all along just waiting for you to start living the life you are suppose to be living. When you can become aware of this you begin to meet people who are in alignment with your passion and new doors of opportunity will open. Please don't be afraid of what is behind these doors. Stepping into the unknown will allow you to open the doors to live the life you are meant to be living. Go ahead, open the door and step on through. It is here that you will discover the passions that have the potential for you to live your life to the fullest.

Living your life of passion in the end will come from within and not from striving for outer appearances, what people will think, or outer circumstances, what is happening to you. Nothing is more important or joyous than living and dancing the life that is uniquely you.

When you are living your life with passion you are quite honestly the richest person on the planet. No amount of gold or money can take its place. And here is the clincher. When you are living your passion, monetary rewards will flow through you more naturally. Your ability to detach will allow you to give more freely and in return gain greater rewards than you have ever thought possible. Just like a boomerang when you give without being attached to the outcome the rewards that come back to you are that much greater.

Go ahead. Align with "what is" instead of "what is not." You are only here a short time. Make the most of it by "living your life with passion."

Inventing the Future

Never before in the history of man have there been so many opportunities and challenges to adapt to. Change is happening faster and faster and the world is growing smaller and smaller as telecommunication technology and the global economy start to integrate. It appears that no corner of the world is being left untouched by our accelerating globalization.

What kind of future do you want to create?

> *"If we were logical, the future would be bleak indeed. But we are more than logical. We are human beings, and we have faith, and we have hope, and we can work."*
> *–Jacques Cousteau–*

Looking into the future can be like exploring the dense woods of Zena along the shores of Grand Lake at night. A combination of unforeseen threats and opportunities confront us as we take each tentative step into the great unknown. Without a map, compass, or guiding light the chances are that, before too long, even the most seasoned explorer can end up lost, stumbling blindly in the dark far from the intended path. Being able to identify your map and plan for the future takes effort and determination. Things that have been rewarded in the past may not be rewarded in the future. In an attempt to support you in adapting to our ever-changing world here are some critical tools that enable me to discover, imagine, and initiate the future I want to create. Simply put a method that allows people to be part of inventing the future.

Openness to Change

It has been said that nothing is sure but change and taxes. Our ability to embrace change can make a major difference in how we evolve our careers, families, personal lives and community. Change is also a sneak peak into the future and for those who can stay calm and centered during times of change, will see through the chaos and new opportunities will become visible.

Foresight into the Future

Today there are more tools and organizations sharing their knowledge on the future than ever before. With these tools you can learn what trends are altering society, economics, the environment, business, and the cultural landscape. The ability see ahead can make the difference between excelling in the future or being left behind.

> *"We ourselves feel that what we are doing is just a drop in the ocean, but the ocean would be less because of that missing drop."*
>
> *—Mother Teresa—*

Insight into New Opportunities

Many people refer to those with insight as lucky because they always seem to be in the right place at the right time. In all reality these people have an ability to see future needs and then meet those needs with new products and/or services.

Flexible Strategy & Execution

James Ogilvy refers to this as Goalessness. This is the ability to adapt to the changing world by embracing new opportunities that enhance your goals and objectives. Very rarely is there a straight path to any desired outcome. Take off the blinders and begin to take in the world with new eyes.

As global issues, world cultures, integrated economies, and technologies continue to change so does our need to think differently. What is holding you back from adapting to our changing world? With fundamental changes happening in every facet of our lives and extending out into the world in which we live, it is becoming more and more critical to alter the way we think about our world.

Looking forward to tomorrow and our next adventure I encourage you to take the time to think about the kind of future you want to create and then go for it. You can do anything you want with a little effort and persistence. Thinking globally and acting locally has become an imperative for the future.

Always a Time for Thanks

Thanksgiving is the time of year family and friends gather to celebrate Thanksgiving, a time set aside to express gratitude for all that has come into our lives. Many of us fill our ovens with as big a bird as we can find. Some fill their bellies to the stretching point and others glue their eyes to the television set to watch football. Some engage in lengthy conversations with one another while others play board games. And some take the time to relax and recharge batteries.

Yet how many of you take the time to contact someone who is not part of your Thanksgiving celebrations: someone that you are thankful for being a part of your life: the person who has influenced you in positive ways, has taken the time to make a difference in your life, and accepts you just as you are. You know, the person in your life you are always wishing you could talk with, but you just don't seem to make the time. Now is the time! Go ahead and make the call, or email the person for whom you are grateful. This kind of gratitude is priceless and only builds positive energy that can last a lifetime.

I am grateful for the times I am able to spent on Grand Lake. There is so much to be thankful for: some of the most dynamic seasonal weather you could ask for, people who care and give so much of themselves to make where we live even better, one of the most incredible lakes on the planet, people who want to help people. It is a place where you can do anything you want to do and more. Absolutely fantastic! I am so grateful for each day that I am able to stand on the shores of such a sacred spot.

Thanksgiving is the time of year that I like to take the time and think about everything that I have to be grateful for. I usually pull out one of my handmade sketch books and start putting down on paper my appreciations for the people, places and things that have influenced my life in a positive way over the years.

Visualizing what I am grateful for is such an inspiring process to go through. It makes me smile. It enables me to relive positive interactions and experiences and reinforce the lessons that I have learned. Yet, why is it that I only tend to do this once a year? Is it because I am continually in the "doing mode?" Is it because I allow my daily activities to take over and I forget what I am grateful for?

How do you express your graditude? Visualizing your appreciations in a journal is a great way to get started.

Sometime in 1989 I started writing down all the things I was grateful for each and every day. I filled journals with what I was grateful for before I would go to sleep each night. At dinner I would ask friends and family what they were grateful for today. It was always interesting to ask people, "What are you grateful for today?" when they were not used to thinking about it. The question forced them to look at the positive and explore what was good in their lives. As time has passed I have lost the intensity of asking myself the question on a regular basis. No more do I write down in my journal what I am grateful for today. Why not?

Life has a way of taking over reducing the amount of time we have to reflect, be still, and give thanks throughout the year. We all have something to be grateful for. This year I am grateful for my continued ability to impact people's lives in positive and inspirational ways. I am grateful for the ability to give back and make a positive difference. I am grateful for having everything I need taken care of. I am grateful for being surrounded by great family and friends. I am grateful for having the fingers and hands that give me the ability to type the words you are reading right now.

What are you grateful for? How are you expressing gratitude in your life?

Every day holds hundreds of opportunities to express your gratitude. Just think how much the world would change for the better if we all started showing more appreciation for the people and things we are grateful for in our lives.

Writing this *What Box?* story has reminded me of how much I can improve the amount of times I share my gratitude and appreciation in my life. And for this I am grateful.

> *"Feeling gratitude and not expressing it is like wrapping*
> *a present and not giving it."*
>
> *—William Arthur Ward—*

How can you express your "thank-you's" on a more regular basis?

One Starfish at a Time

Have you ever heard the story of the man walking down a beach that is covered with starfish as far as the eye can see? In the distance he observes a boy throwing starfish back into the ocean as fast as he can. After walking quite some distance across thousands of starfish he asks the boy, "What are you doing?" "I am saving the starfish from dying," the boy says. The man responds, "Look how many starfish there are. How can you possibly make a difference?" The boy responded without hesitation, "I am making a difference for this one."

One starfish at a time is how he was making a difference and you can too.

I have been like a starfish on more than one occasion. Back in Junior High School I was given one last chance to make it through the traditional learning system after being removed from over eight schools in my educational career. Yes, eight schools. Almost everyone had given up on me. I can still remember sitting outside the principal's office in the 5th grade, for yet another time, when he said, "Sean you will either end up being a multi-millionaire or in jail, because you just seem to want to make your own rules."

The teacher who decided I was worth saving in the eighth grade was Frank Interbitzen and he was hell bent on seeing me make it through at least one level of school without being removed. You see, up to that point I had not even been able to stay enrolled in one class for the entire year, much less my entire schedule of classes without being moved or removed. One day at the beginning of the school year he sat down with my mother and me to discuss what topics interested me. At that time I was totally obsessed by dinosaurs and nature. You know, the kid with dinosaur toys all over the place. He thought for a while and said "Let's enroll Sean in the biology class and see where that takes him." Not even Frank could have been prepared for what happened next.

The school administrator that was already working hard to put me into an alternative education class environment said, "There is no way this kid can be enrolled in the biology class. How can you even think he could perform well when he can't even get through a basic English class, much less biology." With help from my mother, Frank persevered and pushed it all the way to the heads of the school district and put his job on the line in support of this wild-eyed kid.

All of the sudden I was sitting in a biology class with some of the best students in the school. I was very nervous and totally unsure of my self at the time. One of our first projects was to dissect a frog and boy did I take to that like a, well, a frog in water. For the first time that my parents could remember I was studying. All I could think about was my biology class.

To the surprise of all the naysayers, I just could not get enough of that class and even ended up mentoring other students after hours on how to conduct the delicate dissection process. Guess what? I passed the class with my very first "B".

I had done so well that I was one of the top students in the class and nominated as one of twelve students to be in the advanced biology class the following year. In this biology class we would spend a good part of the year dissecting a cat and identifying all the major muscles and other amazing body parts. It was fantastic and I ended up graduating from all two years of Junior High School.

Looking back on that pivotal moment in my life I realize Frank Interbitzen probably saved my life. He did not have to do what he did and it certainly did not look like a good bet from the history he had to go from. In the end he saw something in me that others did not. Except for my mother, he realized that I was not being challenged enough to stay focused on the subjects at hand. Frank, wherever you are now I am so grateful you were willing to throw this starfish back into the ocean of life. There are so many more stories of how Frank kept at it with me, but those will have to wait for another day.

> *"It is well to give when asked, but it is better to give un-asked, through understanding."*
>
> *– Kahlil Gabran–*

The boy throwing the starfish back into the water saw life and death at the physical level. My teacher saw life and death for me at the mental and emotional level. Both enabled life to continue and be enhanced to a greater level.

Where do you see that you can contribute to life enhancing possibilities in the lives that you affect?

Give It Away!

In today's world the perception of scarcity is strong and we tend to hold onto what we have with great tenacity. Some people put their stuff in safes, build fences, fill storage lockers full of unused stuff, while others spend loads of money on alarm systems to increase their feeling of security. Even countries around the world continue to go to the extreme of building huge cement walls to protect their stuff.

In business companies spend billions of dollars each year protecting their ideas, products, and brands. Pharmaceutical corporations are scouring the globe looking for medicines from the roots of plants to the DNA of insects and animals to cure our ills. They go to the most remote villages on the planet to learn from the natives how to create medicines that can cure our illnesses, wisdom that has been passed on from generation to generation. These tribal shamans are more than willing to share their timeless knowledge so that others may be healed. Once shared and with the wisdom and know-how secured, big corporations turn around and patent it so that others can't share in it or own it. Even worse these corporations don't share the monetary rewards generated from this wisdom with the people who gave away their intellectual property.

Some individuals and businesses are starting to realize that holding onto things–ideas, methods, and brands–is an illusion that isn't sustainable. They are realizing that when you give away elements of value you end up gaining more in return. True selflessness and altruism are rare today. Everyone seems to expect something in return for whatever it is they give away. I believe and have experienced in my life, "You reap what you sow." The more I give away the more I receive.

This is not a new idea. In fact it is more of a universal truth. Yet, why is it that people seem to believe so strongly that what they own, their ideas or talents are so valuable that they can't share them with others? Is it because the "idea of giving it away" and actually "doing it" is not so easy? Society has pounded into our heads that when you have an idea or talent you need to protect it. Don't let it out, someone might steal it. This kind of thinking limits our ability to come up with new ideas because people believe "that idea" is the one and only and they don't know if they will be able to come up with another one.

If our founding fathers had this kind of limited thinking I am not sure if we would be where we are today. Benjamin Franklin was always sharing his ideas freely through weekly meetings, the Farmers Almanac and other public speaking engagements. Thomas Jefferson was known for sharing his ideas without abandon. The list of founding fathers willing to share their unique ideas are paramount to what we have become as a nation. What has happened to this willingness to share and to give away for the betterment of others? Why do we put ourselves first and others second?

In my line of work if I am not coming up with new creative and innovative ideas on a regular basis I would be out of business. I regularly instill the following thinking with clients who say, "That is a great idea. I don't know how you are going to top that one." I respond with, "Hey, you like that one, wait 'til we really get cooking. There are a hundred more that are better yet to be discovered." This always blows their minds. Why? Because they think that great ideas are difficult to harvest and that when they find a good one they better hold onto it with all their might. This is a symptom of a scarcity mentality.

Nolan Bushnell, founder of Atari and Chuckie Cheeses Pizza, along with a good friend and mentor of mine, says, "There are no new ideas and it is impossible to protect the ideas you have. Just one modification and it is a different idea." I tend to believe this line of thinking. The whole idea of protecting an idea is very strange and very Western. Leonardo Da Vinci envisioned and drew concepts of helicopter flight 500 years before it became reality. The idea of visiting the moon was something people envisioned hundreds of years before we landed on it. Napoleon developed canned food to feed his troops as they traveled around the world. This method later became the process for creating champagne. Nothing is new, only an innovation of what has been.

Give it away I say. The more you give away the more you get. The more you give away the more your life reaches its fullest potential. The more you give away the more you will support people to reach their full potential. The more you give away the more you will create positive energy in your life. The more you give away the more you will naturally align with the flow of life. The more you give away the more you will enjoy all that is. The more you give away the more meaning you will create in your life. Give it away today! In the end you have to make the decision of giving it away or holding on to it. What will you choose?

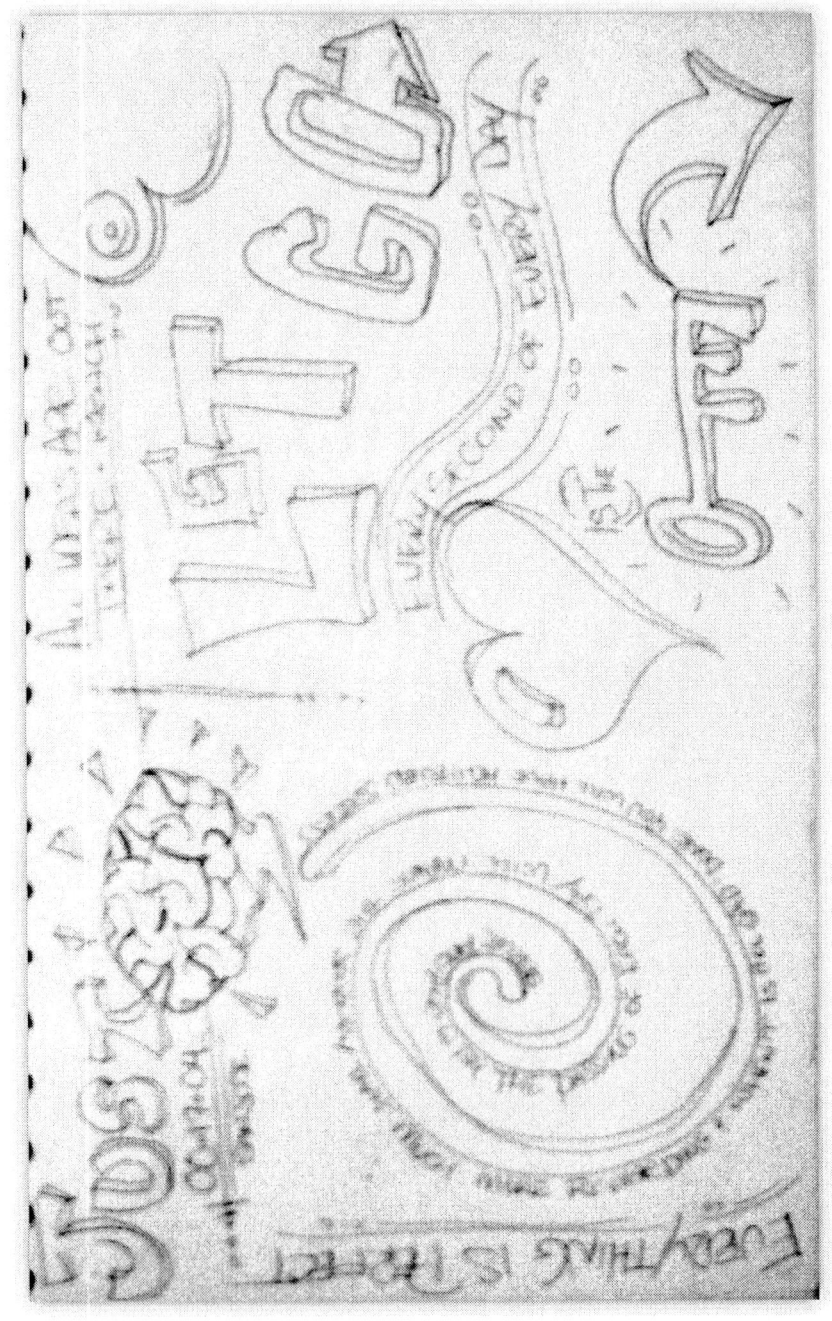

Never Give Up

"When you get into a tight place and everything goes against you, until it seems as though you could not hang on a minute longer, it is then when you should never give up, for that is just the place in time when the tide will turn."

–Harriet Beecher Stowe–

Never Give Up

In my quest to discover what it is I truly want from life and to manifest my mission to "Make a Positive Difference and Show What is Possible," I have stumbled and fallen way more than I have succeeded in achieving my goals. I have found that the more I have stuck myself out there, the more arrows that will be shot into my back. These arrows have held a great influence on me, teaching me new ways to approach whatever it is I have been doing. The challenge for all of us is not only in identifying these new approaches so we can reach our goals, but also to muster the courage to continue in the quest and "Never Give Up."

"If it were easy, everyone would be doing it," is what my buddy, Joe Paul, and I always say to each other, whenever we are exhausted to our last breath from either tearing down an old barn or rebuilding an antique log cabin. The majority of people take the road most traveled, the road down hill. For those few who are willing to trek up the hill and take the road less traveled it is important to nurture a "Never Ever Give Up" attitude in life. The journey of discovery into the unknown is one of the greatest journeys one can pursue, because it has the tremendous potential to transform you into the person you were meant to be.

In my life, the intelligence I inherited, along with my ambitious nature and a strong dedication to immersive learning has resulted in the development of a powerful determination to "Never Give Up." It has not always been easy to embrace the idea of "Never Give Up." Many times in my life I have wanted to just "throw in the towel" on numerous endeavors. In some cases I probably gave up too soon and in others held on too long. Like so many things in life it takes practice, patience, and courage to embrace an attitude of "Never Give Up." Whenever I get down and feel like I can't keep going on with something I am working on, I like to read the following true-life story. It inspires me to keep on keeping on.

Feel discouraged occasionally? The next time discouragement hits you, remember the story of a young man of limited background, possessing little more than a self-administered education. Upon completion of military service, he decided to enter politics by running for a seat in the state legislature. He was soundly defeated. He abandoned politics to try his hand at the storekeeper's trade. The store went bankrupt, and he spent the next 17 years paying off the debt. He fell in love with a woman . . . and suffered the heartbreaking experience of watching her die from typhoid fever. He then spent the next several months bedridden in a state of major depression.

Back on his feet he again decided to enter politics, this time as a candidate for Congress. He was elected by a narrow margin, and when he ran for re-election he was defeated. He also became a candidate for the United States Senate and was defeated. He sought a position with the United States land office and failed to get the job. He was nominated for the Vice Presidency at the Presidential convention of a major political party and lost to a political unknown on the final ballot.

Running again for Senate, he waged a campaign which captured the attention of the nation, but which netted him only defeat once again. Instead of giving up, he continued to dedicate himself to the ideals and principals in which he believed. His eventual reward is familiar to us all, for Abraham Lincoln, although often discouraged during his lifetime, in the end he "Never Gave Up."

Believe and Trust in Yourself

Inside of you is the ability to do and accomplish the most remarkable things. Anything. Everyone, no matter if it is Bill Gates, Oprah Winfrey, George W. Bush, or the neighbor next door, are just like us. They too have to put their pants on one leg at a time.

Some people may have more resources, some may have less, some may have none. Nothing changes the truth that we all have the capacity to achieve great things if we desire and are willing to work hard enough to make our dreams come true. You can do and create anything you can image if you put your mind to it and believe in yourself.

What is it that holds many of us back from doing and achieving the things we want in life? Is it because we are scared to fail? Is it because the goal is perceived to be too much work? Is it because we don't believe we can do it? Or perhaps we are scared of success?

This can be one of the trickiest parts of life's success. When we are young we are all told "NO" a lot, "You can't do that," or the ever-popular "It will never work." This kind of messaging is pounded into our brains so much that many of us start believing in our heart of hearts that we can't do what we know we CAN do. As adults we perpetuate this undermining messaging, telling others that they can't do something, all because of our programming as children. Following this negative and unproductive line of reasoning for yourself will only result in achieving far fewer meaningful accomplishments in your life than if you choose to live a life of "I CAN do anything!"

> *"Become a possibilitarian. No matter how dark things seem to be or actually are, raise your sights and see possibilities–always see them, for they are always there."*
> *–Norman Vincent Peale–*

The challenge is to find the courage not to be influenced by the nay-sayers and to believe deep down inside that you can accomplish anything no matter what people might say. What if the Wright Brothers had listened to all the people who said, "You'll never be able to fly." Instead, they chose to believe they could. When you are able to believe that you can do anything, it does not mean that your life will result in instant accomplishments. Success comes in small steps, in small accomplishments that eventually add up to big accomplishments, big successes. It is said that every overnight success takes 20 years. The Wright Brothers had to work very hard and experiment many, many times along the journey to human flight. They never ever gave up and continued believing they could and would fly. Just like the Wright Brothers you have everything you need inside of you to reach your dreams. It is never too late to start.

> *"Every achiever that I have ever met says, my life turned around when I began to believe in me."*
> —*Robert H. Schuller*—

In so many cases people believe that they will not succeed even before they start something. What a travesty. Instead, create a mindset of expecting success even before you start. All achievers, no matter what their game, start with the expectations that they are going to succeed. Achievers say, "I want to do this and I CAN do this," not "I would like to do this, but I don't think I can."

What do you think about yourself and your abilities?

Say you CAN and you WILL. Say you CAN'T and you WON'T. This is a universal truth we can't hide from.

Try this. Next week become a Possibilitarian and say YES to those things that the week before you said NO to. Say "I CAN do this," "We CAN do this" and see what happens.

You CAN and WILL do what you think you CAN.

> *"Believe in yourself and you will be unstoppable!"*
> —*Emily Guay*—

Never, Ever Give Up

For me there is nothing much better than a "blank canvas" whether or not it is a large piece of paper, a living area, a boat dock or the walls of a building. The process of transforming a blank space into a visually dynamic space that inspires greater thinking is very energizing. I gravitate towards large scale mural projects that support building team and community spirit.

A transformation of the staircase at the Miami Family Crisis Center's Resale Shop took place with the addition of one of my new murals, A Smiling Hero. The mural is a vibrant and colorful tribute to the strength and heart associated with running a crisis center. A Smiling Hero was sketched on the staircase walls and ws painted by the Crisis Center team. lead by Deedee Cox.

It is hard to believe that the Smiling Hero mural, the grand opportunity to add color, emotion, and team spirit almost did not happen. The mural was originally auctioned off at a fundraising for the Crisis Center in 2002. Tom Sanders paid for a wall to be built, Jeff Lundgren paid for the paint supplies and I donated my time as the artist to design and paint the mural. As time went by, changes were made in the layout of the Crisis Center Resale Shop and meeting rooms, creating limited wall space for the mural. One of the alternative possibilities that was discussed was that I could paint the mural on the outside of the Crisis Center walls. This idea started to move forward.

Over the past few years I have worked with the team to harvest their visions of what the mural could be. Studies were generated, multiple proposals were developed, and numerous presentations were made to the Crisis Center Board, Miami Community Leaders, and the Miami Chamber of Commerce. It is important to note that going into this project I knew that any kind of mural project involving many different perspectives was going to take time in order to build consensus. The excitement and scope of the project grew into a multi-wall mural project which would involve the entire Miami community in painting the murals. Things were really cooking and then they came to a stand still. My other activities and endeavors started to consume more and more of my time and I began to think that this artistic community building project would not happen. I felt that I had done all I could do to facilitate a process to enable people to come together and reach consensus on this project. I had been attached to this happening and realized that I needed to back off and let things happen as they would.

> *"Never give up! Failure and rejection are only the first step to succeeding."*
>
> *—Jimmy Valvano—*

It is interesting that when you let something go, you start to detach from the outcome, allowing new possibilities to take form. That is what happened in this situation. At the beginning of the year Deedee got in touch with me and said, "I have a wall for you. When can you paint it?" I thought to myself, "never, ever give-up." The concept of the project was correct, it just didn't happen in the time frame that I had planned.

So now I am thinking about the possibility of transforming other walls around the world. You just never know. We have a good start. It takes a lot of patience and intestinal fortitude to never ever give up on what ever it is you are doing. It is important to remain flexible and learn to work with people and their unique perspectives and gifts.

> *"What this power is I cannot say. All I know is that it exists and it becomes available only when a man is in that state of mind in which he knows exactly what he wants and is fully determined not to quit until he finds it."*
>
> *—Alexander Graham Bell—*

Bibliography

Anderson, Peggy. *Great Quotes from Great Leaders*. Pleasantville, NY: The Careers Press, Inc., 1997.

Buzan, Tony and Barry Buzan. *The Mind Map Book*. New York: A Dutton Book, 1990.

Cameron, Julia. *The Artist's Way*. New York: Penguin Putnam, Inc., 1992.

Canfield, Jack and Mark Victor Hansen. *Chicken Soup for the Soul*. Florida: Health Communications, Inc., 1993.

Castaneda, Carlos. *Journey To Ixtlan*. New York: Washington Square Press, 1991.

Covey, Stephen. *The Seven Habits of Highly Effective People*. New York: Simon & Schuster, 1989.

De Bono, Edward. *Six Thinking Hats: The Power of Focused Thinking*. MICA Management Resources, Inc., 1999.

Edison, Lee. *How We Learn*. New York: Pocket Books, 1975.

Shakti Gawain. *Creative Visualization: Use the Power of Your Imagination to Create What You Want in Your Life*. Navato: Nataraj Publishing, 2002.

Hanks, K. and L. Belliston. *Draw! A Visual Approach to Thinking, Learning and Communication*. Los Altos, CA: William Kaufman, 1977.

Hill, Napolean and W. Clement Stone. *Success Through a Positive Mental Attitude*. New York: Pocket Books, 1977.

Klein, Allen. *The Change-Your-Life Quote Book*. New York: Gramercy Books, 2000.

Lamay, Leo and P.M. Zall. *Benjamin Franklin's Autobiography*. New York: W.W. Norton and Co., 1986.

Miner, Margaret and Hugh Rawson. *The New International Dictionary of Quotations–Third Edition.* USA: New American Library, 2000.

Rathbun, Harry J. *Creative Initiative–Guide To Fulfillment.* Palo Alto, CA: Creative Initiative Foundation, 1976.

Reader's Digest. *Reader's Digest Quotable Quotes.* Pleasantville, NY: The Reader's Digest Association, Inc., 1997.

Rico, Gabriele Lusser. *Writing the Natural Way.* Pleasantville, NY: G.P. Putnam's Sons, 1983.

Sibbet, David. *I See What You Mean.* San Francisco, CA: Sibbett & Associates, 1980.

Toile, Eckhart. *The Power of Now.* Novato, CA: New World Library, 1999.

Vienne, Veronuque. *The Art of Doing Nothing.* New York: Clarkson Potter/ Publisher, 1998.

Vilord, Thomas J. *1001 Motivational Quotes for Success–Great Quotes from Great Minds.* Cherry Hill, NJ: Garden State Publishing, 2004.

Yates, F. A. *The Art of Memory.* London: Routledge & Kegan Paul, 1984.

Young, Chesley V. *The Magic of a Mighty Memory.* New York: Parker Publishing Co., 1971.

Zukav, Gary. *The Seat of the Soul.* New York: Simon & Schuster, 1989.

Ted Andrews. *Animal Speak: The Spiritual & Magical Powers of Creatures Great & Small.* St. Paul, MN: Llewellyn Publications, 2004.

Norman Vincent Peale. *The Power of Positive Thinking.* New York: Random House, 1952.

Paramahansa Yogananda. *Autobiography of a Yogi.* Los Angeles, CA: Self-Realization Fellowship Publishers, 1979.